THE RISE AND FALL
OF
SAN DIEGO

GEOLOGIC TIME SCALE			
ERA	**PERIOD**	**EPOCH**	**Millions of Years Ago**
CENOZOIC	QUATERNARY	Holocene	0.011
		Pleistocene	1.8 (2.67)
	TERTIARY	Pliocene	5.3
	NEOGENE	Miocene	23.8
	PALEOGENE	Oligocene	33.7
		Eocene	55
		Paleocene	65
MESOZOIC	CRETACEOUS	Late	99
		Early	142
	JURASSIC	Late	
		Middle	
		Early	205.7
	TRIASSIC	Late	
		Middle	
		Early	250
PALEOZOIC	PERMIAN	Late	
		Early	290
	CARBONIFEROUS PENNSYLVANIAN	Late	323
	MISSISSIPPIAN	Early	354
	DEVONIAN	Late	
		Middle	
		Early	417
	SILURIAN	Late	
		Early	443
	ORDOVICIAN	Late	
		Middle	
		Early	495
	CAMBRIAN	Late	
		Middle	
		Early	545
PRECAMBRIAN			
ORIGIN OF EARTH			4,550

PATRICK L. ABBOTT

THE RISE AND FALL
OF
SAN DIEGO

150 MILLION YEARS OF HISTORY
RECORDED IN
SEDIMENTARY ROCKS

Sunbelt Natural History Books
"Adventures in the Natural and Cultural History
of the Californias"

A series edited by Lowell Lindsay

SUNBELT PUBLICATIONS
San Diego, California

Sunbelt Publications, Inc.
P.O. Box 191126
San Diego, CA 92159-1126
(935) 258-4911 (935) 258-4916 fax (Area Code 619 until June 2000)
www.sunbeltpub.com

"Sunbelt Natural History Books"
A series edited by Lowell Lindsay

04 03 02 00 99 5 4 3 2 1

Library of Congress Cataloging-in-Publication Data

Abbott, Patrick L.
    The Rise and Fall of San Diego: 150 million years of history recorded
    in sedimentary rocks/Patrick L. Abbott.
        p. cm.--(Sunbelt natural history guides)

    Includes bibliographical references and index.
    ISBN 0-932653-31-6
    First Edition 1999

    1. Geology--California--San Diego Region. 2. Geology, Stratigraphic.
    3. Geology--California--San Diego Region Guidebooks. 4. San Diego
    Region (Calif.) Guidebooks. I. Title. II. Series.

QE90.A117A23 1999   99-35670
557.94'98--dc21   CIP

CONTENTS

PREFACE

Reading sedimentary rocks is like reading a history book, with each rock layer, like a page in a book, revealing fascinating stories from the past. *The Rise and Fall of San Diego* was written for the nongeologist, and it tells the 150-million-year history of the San Diego area recorded in sedimentary rock layers. A vast amount of information about past events and ancient life forms is contained within them. *The Rise and Fall of San Diego* is the history of the sedimentary rocks in San Diego and the fossils they contain—the key to interpreting this history lies in learning how to read the rocks.

The land has risen and fallen, and independently so have sea levels; combined they have created a changing landscape that has affected the changing life forms that have lived here. Have you ever wondered, for example, as you walked south along the beach in Torrey Pines State Reserve and looked up at the massive cliff face, why some layers are orangish while others are greenish, why some layers have fossils and others do not? Have you waded through the tidepools at Point Loma and wondered what caused the intricate patterns and delicate trace fossils you see in the rock beds? In *The Rise and Fall of San Diego* you will find the answers to these and many other questions; you will also learn how geologists gather information and put the data together into a geologic history.

What philosophy underlies the data collection and hypothesis formation described in this book? Any motivated individual can make significant contributions to geologic and paleontologic knowledge if they work within a few guidelines:

- Have a genuine respect for truth, and collect and evaluate all data critically.
- Hypotheses that seek to explain must account for *all* data; avoid picking and choosing only the data that support your hypothesis.
- Avoid becoming emotionally attached to any hypothesis. Hypotheses are made as approximations of the truth, and they serve merely to guide us through the next wave of data collection. Keep in mind that hypotheses are designed to be disproved; the ever-evolving scientific search for truth is a ruthless slayer of pet theories.

If you are willing to follow these guidelines, you will find a lifetime's worth of intriguing problems to investigate. Searching for data, forming hypotheses, and rigorously evaluating both are consuming passions that add meaning and a sense of accomplishment to life. Furthermore, developing an ability to "read" the rocks does *not* require a college degree in geology; in fact, some of the people cited in the text for their significant geologic and paleontologic contributions are not geologists nor even college graduates, though they all abide by the rules for scientific inquiry. Science has the great advantage of being self-correcting; poor data and faulty hypotheses eventually pale in the light of good data and honest analysis.

The information contained here represents the work of many people over many years, and to give you a feel for the collective effort involved in data collection and interpretation I have included the names of some of the individuals who have played significant roles in the ongoing investigation. I have also included references to some of the scientific literature containing the work of other significant contributors. However, because of space limitations many names and citations have, by necessity, been left out, and I apologize for these omissions.

Throughout *The Rise and Fall of San Diego* I have eliminated scientific jargon wherever possible in an effort to make the discussion accessible to nonscientists. For those who are interested in geology and motivated to work through the material in the book and the field trips, the information presented here will provide insight and understanding into San Diego's fascinating geologic history. For additional information about terminology, geologic processes, and overall geologic history, a number of useful books are listed at the end of the first chapter as well as in the reference list at the end of the book.

Acknowledgments

Tom Deméré made valuable contributions to some of the paleontology sections and read most of the manuscript. Deméré and his colleagues at the San Diego Museum of Natural History in Balboa Park are the leaders in paleontologic research in the San Diego region. Rene Wagemakers drafted many of the figures that are so important in understanding this geologic history; I owe him much for his labor and talent. Christina MacPhail used her talents to read and edit the entire text, and the book has been improved by her efforts. Mike Walawender read and commented on some of the early chapters. Marie Ayers and Pia Parrish provided valuable help with the tables.

Finally, I gratefully acknowledge all the individuals in the 19th and 20th centuries who have given us so much insight into the geologic history of San Diego. I invite all readers to lend their energies and talents in the 21st century to the ongoing effort to increase our understanding of geologic history. Local individuals whose contributions are mentioned in the text include:

Liz Baker, Duane Balch, Bill Bartling, Sarah Bartling, Dick Berry, Steve Borron, Dave Bukry, Richard Cerutti, Nancy Cox, Perry Crampton, Scott Curran, W. H. Dall, Marlene Dean, Tom Deméré, Roy Dokka, Will Elder, Bill Elliott, Arthur Ellis, H. W. Fairbanks, Eric Frost, Melissa Girty, Ulysses S. Grant IV, Bob Gutzler, Dennis Hannan, Colleen Haradan, Chuck Herzig, Kenji Hirabayashi, Mike Kennedy, Phil Kern, Dennis Kerr,

Ron Kies, Dave Kimbrough, Dan Krummenacher, Mark Legg, Scott Lindvall, Pablo Lopez, Dick McCarthy, Paul Majors, Jim Mattinson, Jeff May, Jay Melosh, Richard Merriam, Rick Miller, John Minch, George Moore, Tor Nilsen, Chuck Nord strom, J. D. Obradovich, Gary Peterson, Don Prothero, E. H. Quayle, Brad Riney, Tom Rockwell, Mark Roeder, Gary Simpson, Bill Sliter, Judy Terry Smith, Terry Smith, Brad Steer, Charlie Stuart, Don Swanson, Lee Vanderhurst, Steve Walsh, E. E. Welday, Charlie Winker, A. O. Woodford, and Eli Zlotnik.

FIGURES AND TABLES

Chapter 3

Chapter 4

Chapter 5

Chapter 6

Chapter 7

Chapter 8

Chapter 9

CHAPTER 1
ROCKS AND TIME

Introduction

Historians describe the modern history of San Diego as beginning on 28 September 1542, when Portuguese-born explorer Juan Rodriguez Cabrillo first sailed into San Diego Bay. Continuous European settlement is usually dated from 16 July 1769 when the Franciscan friar Junipero Serra gave the first mass on Presidio Hill in Old Town. For those who dig deeper into history, the archaeological record in San Diego reaches further back in time. Some 11,000 years ago, peoples of the San Dieguito culture thrived here, followed by those of the La Jollan culture, who in turn were supplanted 2,000 years ago by peoples of the Kumeyaay culture. The Kumeyaay were here when Cabrillo arrived, and their descendants live here still.

The history of San Diego can also be read from sedimentary rocks, extending our knowledge much deeper into the past, back some 150 million years. Before carefully "reading" the rocks of San Diego to learn some of this geologic history, we first need to understand how topography is formed and destroyed, how sediments and fossils are deposited and preserved, and how the ages of rocks and fossils can be determined.

Plate Tectonics

The flow of energy from the Earth's interior to the surface is visible in our lifetimes as volcanic eruptions and earthquakes. Over geologic time, the energy flow opens and closes ocean basins in the process of *plate tectonics*. Hot, buoyant rock and magma rise up from the Earth's mantle, breaking through the brittle lithosphere to build volcanoes in continuous mountain ranges that circle the Earth (Figure 1.1). The injection of magma creates high-standing volcanic mountains that are pulled apart by gravity to form spreading centers, which continuously form new sea floor in conveyer-belt fashion. The rising magma helps to force apart the lithosphere (ridge push), and gravity pulls apart the volcanic mountains, creating gigantic slabs (plates). The lithospheric plates are about 60 miles thick and hundreds of miles across. The plates are pulled apart by gravity (slab pull) forming ever-opening ocean basins in the process known as *sea-floor spreading*. The massive, moving plates (1) pull apart at spreading centers (such as the Gulf of California), (2) slide past each other (such as along the San Andreas fault), or (3) collide at

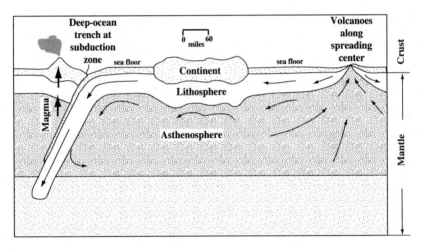

Figure 1.1. Cross-sectional (vertical slice) view of plate tectonics. Magma rises to build volcanic mountains at spreading centers. Gravity pulls the spreading center apart in huge plates of lithosphere that slide on top of the asthenosphere. Where lithospheric plates collide, a dense plate will bend down into the asthenosphere in the process of subduction.

subduction zones (such as the Aleutian Islands of Alaska). The collision of a dense ocean-floor plate with a less dense continent results in the denser oceanic plate turning down into the mantle below the continent in the process of subduction. The leading edge of a subducting oceanic plate bends downward, forming deep trenches on the sea floor.

The interior of the Earth contains huge amounts of heat in its liquid outer core, and the continual decay of radioactive elements adds fuel to the furnace. The internal energy of the Earth can be viewed as fueling the "forces of construction" that form and build topography. Volcanic eruptions build mountains and plateaus; continents riding on moving sea floors collide and stack up into tall mountains and broad plateaus (such as the Himalayas and the Tibetan Plateau). Low-density minerals brought to the surface by the action of volcanoes accumulate and remain at the surface as continents, which literally float on top of the denser rock below. The internal energy of the Earth concentrates to form new spreading centers that tear continents apart, push them around, and recombine them into different shapes during the process of plate tectonics. The land surface rises to form mountain ranges and falls to form basins, and through it all the low-density continental rocks do not sink back into the Earth's interior but just keep floating.

Rock Cycle

Rocks form and transform in an endless cycle over time. Geologists categorize rocks into three major groups—igneous, sedimentary, and metamorphic—depending on how they are made (Figure 1.2).

The internal energy of the Earth causes rock to melt into magma. Hot, buoyant magma rises toward the surface; some magma cools miles below the Earth's surface, forming *plutonic igneous rock* (also known as intrusive rock), and some magma cools when it reaches the Earth's surface, forming *volcanic igneous rock* (also known as extrusive rock). Rocks near the Earth's surface are broken down through mechanical and chemical weathering. *Mechanical weathering* (physical disintegration) occurs, for example, when near-surface rocks are broken down into gravel- and sand-sized particles by plant-root wedging, ice-crystal growth and thaw, and expansion

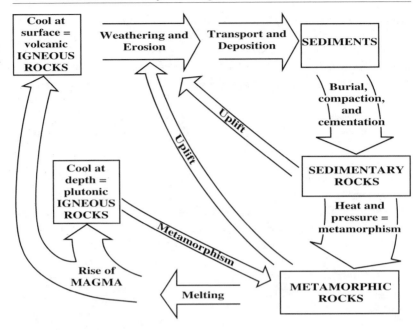

*Figure 1.2. The rock cycle. Magma rises; some cools deep under-
ground, forming plutonic igneous rocks, and some cools on the
surface, forming volcanic igneous rocks. Rocks exposed at the
surface disintegrate and decompose during weathering; loose
debris is carried away by the agents of erosion and deposited in
topographically low places as sediments, which accumulate and
are compressed into sedimentary rocks by the pressure of deep
burial. If burial continues, the increasing temperature and pressure transform the sedimentary rocks into metamorphic rocks.*

caused by solar heating followed by contraction on cooling. *Chemical
weathering* (chemical decomposition) occurs, for example, when rocks
at or near the surface are decomposed by water that has been charged
with carbon dioxide absorbed from the atmosphere and the soil zone
(forming carbonic acid). Chemical decomposition of rocks forms tiny
clay minerals. The sediments (gravel, sand, and clay) produced by
the combined effects of mechanical and chemical weathering are

carried downhill by running water and glaciers as well as by gravity directly. The sediments accumulate in topographic low spots (such as lakes, bays, and oceans). They harden into *sedimentary rock* through (1) *compaction,* which occurs as sediments become more deeply buried; and (2) *cementation,* which occurs as salts crystallize from underground water to bind the sediment grains together. If burial of the sediments continues, the increasing temperature and pressure can metamorphose (change) sedimentary rock minerals into new crystal structures of high-temperature and high-pressure metamorphic minerals, thus forming *metamorphic rocks.*

See the grand interplay that occurs as the internal energy of the Earth creates magmas that crystallize into igneous rocks. But then the external energy from the Sun powers the agents of erosion that break down igneous and other surface rocks and carry them away as debris. From a larger perspective, the topography created by Earth's internal energy is eroded and destroyed by the external energy of the Sun aided by gravity. The solar- and gravity-powered "forces of destruction" continually erode the land and dump the remains into the seas. If Earth's outflow of internal energy were not continually building new landmasses, erosion would destroy all the continents in about 45 million years. For over 4 billion years, mountains have risen and eroded while the rock cycle has operated, all under the same physical laws and processes.

Sedimentary Rocks

As the rock cycle shows, igneous and metamorphic rocks exposed at the Earth's surface are continually subjected to mechanical and chemical weathering, eventually being reduced into loose sediment. Geologists refer to these sediments as gravels, sands, or muds and classify them by grain-size, as shown in Figure 1.3. Sedimentary rocks are named based on the grain size of the dominant sediment; for example, a sedimentary rock dominated by fist-sized gravels is called a *cobble conglomerate,* and a rock made of cemented sand grains is called a *sandstone.* The name *sandstone* modified by its dominant sand-grain size yields a name such as *medium sandstone.*

Geologists interpret sedimentary rocks based on an approach first used by the Scotsman James Hutton in 1785. Hutton observed

Sediment Sizes and Names

Grain Diameter (Millimeters)	Grain-Size Name		Sedimentary Rock Name
	Boulder		
256 (≈10 inches)	- - - - - - - - - -	G	
	Cobble	R	
64 (≈2.5 inches)	- - - - - - - - - -	A	Conglomerate
	Pebble	V	
4 (≈0.16 inch)	- - - - - - - - - -	E	
	Granule	L	
2	---		
	Very coarse		
1	- - - - - - - - - - - - - - - - - -		
	Coarse	S	
0.5	- - - - - - - - - - - - - - - - - -	A	Sandstone
	Medium	N	
0.25	- - - - - - - - - - - - - - - - -	D	
	Fine		
0.125	- - - - - - - - - - - - - - - - -		
	Very Fine		
0.0625	---		
	Silt	M	Siltstone (>2/3 silt)
0.0039	- - - - - - - - - - - - - - - - -	U	
	Clay	D	Mudstone (subequal silt & clay) Claystone (>2/3 clay)

Figure 1.3. Sediment sizes based on the scale developed by J. A. Udden in 1898. Names of size classes were standardized by C. K. Wentworth in 1922.

that the solidified and tilted layers of sandstone he found on hillsides near his home contained the same assortment of sediment sizes and internal structures that he found in modern stream sediments. He inferred from these observations that the hard, tilted beds of sandstone had originally accumulated as sediments in an ancient stream. This style of investigation is called *uniformitarianism* or *actualism*; another way of saying this is, "the present is the key to the past." It involves using our understanding of modern Earth processes and laws of nature to interpret the prehistoric past we find preserved in rocks and fossils.

At San Diego State University (SDSU), I have used this approach for over a quarter of a century in my Sedimentology classes for geology majors. Each class ventures into the field armed with shovels to dig trenches in modern-day beaches, tidal flats, alluvial fans, streams, and wind-blown dunes. Students describe the sediments in each trench in their notebooks and collect samples to take back to the university for laboratory analyses. This style of study allows students to see for themselves the differences among a variety of modern-day sediments in a variety of environments. The better we understand what types of sediments form in each modern environment, the better we can read sedimentary rocks and interpret their contained geologic history.

Sediments and sedimentary rocks contain not only pieces of preexisting rocks but also the remains and traces of early life forms, that is, fossils. For example, the flood waters that spill out of a stream and deposit sand and mud in protected low places may also bury the bones of vertebrate animals, tree leaves, and snail shells. Fossils in sedimentary rocks help us to interpret the environmental conditions at the time the sediment was deposited and the organisms died. The collective sequence of fossils worldwide, the fossil record, covers more than 3.5 billion years of life history on Earth.

Depositional Environments of Sediments

Where are sediments deposited? Are sediments accumulating in all areas of Earth's surface? Do topographically high areas receive as much deposition as low areas? Topographically high areas do not accumulate significant deposits of sediments; instead they shed sediments through weathering and erosion downslope to low-lying areas, such as alluvial fans extending from the base of mountains (Figure 1.4a), river valleys and lakes (Figure 1.4b), coastal plains (beaches, deltas, lagoons, bays, and estuaries) (Figure 1.4c), and ocean basins (including continental shelves, submarine canyons, and submarine fans built at the base of continental slopes and large faults).

Figure 1.4. Sediments accumulate in a variety of depositional environments from near their bedrock mountain sources to deep ocean floors. (a) Alluvial fans are built of coarse sediments that accumulate at the base of steep mountains, such as along the Santa Rosa Mountains in California; (b) river channels and valleys hold large volumes of sand and mud, as along the Sweetwater River, Wyoming; photo by W. R. Hansen, U.S. Geological Survey; (c) the Mission Bay area, although modified by human actions, shows a variety of depositional environments: river delta, bay, barrier beach, shallow marine shelf, and deeper ocean waters receiving sediments via a river.

Figure 1.4a

Figure 1.4b

Figure 1.4c

Some Principles of Sedimentary Rocks

Great thinkers through thousands of years have supplied insights and knowledge that are still valuable today in many fields such as politics and government, drama and psychology, and warfare. However, an understanding of how the Earth works has come relatively late to the human race. The first principles still of value today were set forth by the Dane Nils Steensen, who used the Latin name Steno. In 1669, Steno laid out the *law of superposition,* which states that younger layers of sediment are deposited on top of older layers. Thus in an undisturbed sequence of sedimentary rocks, the lowest layer is the oldest, and each successive layer is younger. Steno's *law of original horizontality* tells us that sediments are initially deposited in near-horizontal layers, thus forming a reference point for understanding later forces that tilted and folded the sedimentary rock layers.

The layers of sedimentary rock at any one place on Earth do not contain a continuous and unbroken record of geologic history. At a particular location, times of sediment deposition alternate with times of nondeposition, and erosion skews the record by removing previously deposited sediments and sedimentary rocks. These breaks in the sedimentary rock record are called *unconformities*. In our quest to understand Earth's history, unconformities represent the loss of a tremendous amount of rock and fossil data which could have been read and interpreted.

Geologic Time

How are the ages of rocks and fossils determined? We have discovered three main methods so far. (1) The first method discovered for measuring geologic time is based on the sequence of fossils found in sedimentary rock layers worldwide. The fossils occur in a unique and irreversible order. This method was first used in the late 1700s and early 1800s. Several decades later, scientists realized that the unique sequence of fossils reflects the history of organic evolution. (2) A second method for recognizing time appeared in the early 1900s after the discovery of radioactivity. Scientists realized that by measuring the amounts of radioactive elements and their decay products locked inside minerals, you could determine when the minerals crystallized from magma, that is, you can measure the age of a rock. (3) The third method for determining past time arose in the 1960s after scientists recognized that the polarity of Earth's magnetic field has flip-flopped from north to south and back again in the course of Earth's history. These magnetic polarity reversals form a unique sequence that is measurable in rocks and has been organized into a third time scale.

GEOLOGIC TIME SCALE BASED ON THE FOSSIL RECORD

The quest to measure the age of rocks took a big step forward in 1799 when the Englishman William Smith, building on Steno's principles of superposition and on the growing knowledge of fossils contained in sedimentary rocks, described the *law of faunal assemblages.* This law explains how groups of sedimentary rock layers can be recognized over wide areas by the unique assemblages of fossils they contain. Smith used faunal assemblages to make geologic maps showing the distribution of rock bodies of equivalent ages.

Combining the laws of superposition and faunal assemblages led to the *law of faunal succession,* which states that fossils found in older rock layers (lower by superposition) are more distinct from present-day organisms than fossils found in younger rock layers (higher by superposition). Faunal succession demonstrates the irreversible sequence of individual first appearances and extinctions of millions of different species worldwide. Motivated by the significance of this principle, geologists worldwide examined their own geographic regions to determine the vertical sequence of fossils contained there. By integrating the results of these findings, geologists compiled a global order of fossil succession that grew into a standardized global sequence by 1841 (Figure 1.5).

GEOLOGIC TIME MEASURED FROM RADIOACTIVE ELEMENT DECAY

We know geologic time in absolute years only from measurements made on radioactive elements and their decay products. For example, the isotope uranium-238 (U-238) decays to lead-206 (Pb-206) in a sequence of emissions where 32 of the 238 subatomic particles in the U-238 nucleus are ejected, thus slimming the nucleus down to the 206 particles of a Pb-206 atom. The rate of decay from U-238 to

EON	ERA		PERIOD		MILLIONS OF YEARS AGO	MAJOR APPEARANCES
PHANEROZOIC	CENOZOIC		QUATERNARY			Humans
					1.8	
			TERTIARY			Direct human ancestors
					65	Flowering plants in abundance
	MESOZOIC		CRETACEOUS			
					142	
			JURASSIC			
					206	Birds
			TRIASSIC			Mammals and dinosaurs
					250	
	PALEOZOIC		PERMIAN			
					290	
		CARBON-IFEROUS	PENNSYLVANIAN			
					323	Reptiles
			MISSISSIPPIAN			
					354	Amphibians
			DEVONIAN			(vertebrates on land)
					417	
			SILURIAN			
					443	
			ORDOVICIAN			Land plants
					495	
			CAMBRIAN			Fishes
					545	Great diversification and abundance of life in the sea
PRE-CAMBRIAN	PROTEROZOIC				1,000	Sexual reproduction
					2,500	
	ARCHEAN				3,600	Oldest fossils
					4,000	Oldest Earth rocks
HADEAN					4,550	Origin of Earth

Figure 1.5. Geologic time scale based on the worldwide sequence of fossils. Numerical ages in absolute years were derived from radioactive element analyses.

Pb-206 has been measured in the laboratory as having a half-life of 4.5 billion years. A half-life is the length of time it takes for half of an existing volume of radioactive atoms to decay. The decay process follows a negative exponential path—that is, one volume goes to one-half in the first half-life, one-half goes to one-quarter in the second half-life, one-quarter goes to one-eighth in the third half-life, and so on.

How do geologists measure the age of a rock using this knowledge? We may, for example, crush a plutonic igneous rock and pick out the zircon crystals. The zircons are then crushed, dissolved under ultraclean conditions, and placed in a mass spectrometer to measure the amounts of U-238 and decay product Pb-206 that are present. Then with three known values—(1) the half-life of U-238 as measured in the laboratory, (2) the amount of U-238 present, and (3) the amount of Pb-206 present—it is easy to calculate a fourth value, the date when the zircon crystal formed by growing in an ancient magma. In other words, the age of the rock has been measured.

GEOLOGIC TIME MEASURED BY POLARITY REVERSALS OF EARTH'S MAGNETIC FIELD

When you hold a compass you can watch its free-turning needle point toward Earth's magnetic pole, which lies near the Earth's north pole of rotation. Has Earth's magnetic pole always been in the same place? The answer is no. Earth's magnetic pole has flip-flopped from north to south and back again at irregular intervals measured in thousands or millions of years.

Earth's magnetic field affects iron-rich minerals in cooling magmas, lining them up with the magnetic pole of their time. Thus the magnetic polarity of the Earth at the time rocks containing these minerals were formed is locked inside the rocks. These rocks can then be dated using their radioactive elements, resulting in known lengths of time for each north and south polarity. Because the magnetic poles switch at unpredictable times, the time intervals between north and south polarities are random; this forms a unique pattern. In Figure 1.6 inspect the nonrepeating pattern of magnetic polarities. When magnetic polarity measurements are calibrated with radiometric ages determined on the same rocks, a third time scale is created—the magnetic polarity-reversal time scale.

Sedimentary Rocks in San Diego

While the processes of plate tectonics are continually creating and elevating the landmasses, the agents of erosion are reducing and eliminating them and dumping the sediment debris into the ocean basins. This dynamic battle between elevation and elimination of land is recorded in sedimentary rocks.

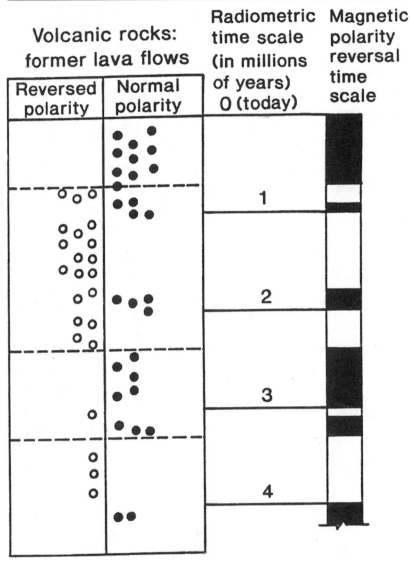

*Figure 1.6. Geologic time scale based on magnetic-polarity re-
versals and their duration. Normal polarity (shown in black)
is to the north; reverse polarity (white) is to the south.*

If we were to zero in on San Diego and watch it through geologic time, we would see intervals of millions of years when the land stood high and no sediments were able to accumulate, leaving no record for us to examine. During other intervals of millions of years, we would see that lands were topographically low and received thick volumes of sediments containing fossils that tell us the history of their time. And so, because these intervals alternate over time, the sedimentary rock record of San Diego is *discontinuous*; in other words, it contains sequences of thick sedimentary rocks separated by erosional unconformities. The Earth is 4.55 billion years old, but only the most recent 150 million years of sedimentary rock is found in San Diego (Figure 1.7). Why is this so? Because San Diego sits on the edge of the growing North American continent and thus has only geologically younger rocks.

What story is told by the sedimentary rocks of San Diego? We could begin by saying that 150–80 million years ago, active subduction of an oceanic plate beneath San Diego fed enormous volumes of magma into the region, yielding the mountainous topography of the ancestral Peninsular Ranges and thus creating few topographically low spots where sediments could be deposited and preserved. During the last 80 million years, the plate-tectonic processes dominating the San Diego area changed in character and shifted to a process called *transform (horizontal-offset) faulting*, which dominates us still. During this last 80 million years, topographically low areas in San Diego have received huge volumes of sediments.

It is now time to begin reading the details of this history stored in the sedimentary rocks and fossils. The following chapters will proceed chronologically from 150 million years ago up to the last million years.

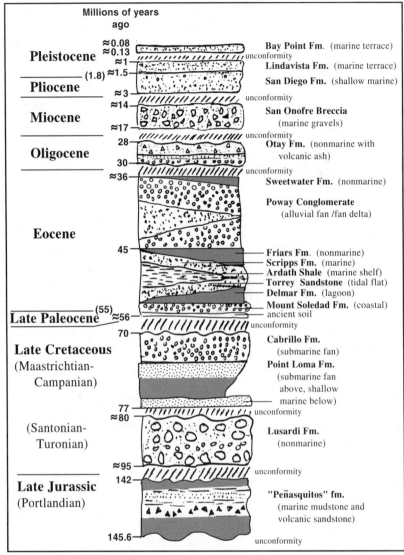

Figure 1.7. The generalized column of sedimentary rocks in the San Diego coastal region showing formation names, depositional environments, and ages derived from radioactive elements.

Further Reading

The preceding introduction to plate tectonics, sedimentary rocks, depositional environments, and geologic time was necessarily brief. For fuller treatments of these topics, please refer to the following books:

Press, Frank, and Raymond Siever, *Earth*. 4th ed. San Francisco: W.H. Freeman, 1995. Excellent introduction to physical geology.

Levin, Harold, *The Earth Through Time*. 5th ed. Fort Worth, Texas: Harcourt Brace College Publishers, 1995. Well-presented introduction to historical geology.

Cowen, Richard, *History of Life*. 2nd ed. London: Blackwell Scientific, 1994. Good overview of the fossil record.

Abbott, Patrick, *Natural Disasters*. 2nd ed. Boston: WCB/McGraw Hill, 1999. Offers an understanding of Earth processes as viewed through natural disasters.

CHAPTER 2
JURASSIC HISTORY

Many of the first geologic and paleontologic studies took place in Europe, and because Jurassic-age rocks (which formed 205.7 to 142 million years ago) are common in Europe, many of these studies dealt with the rocks of this time. In 1799 Alexandre von Humboldt, a German naturalist, traveler, and statesman, described Jurassic-age rocks found in the Jura Mountains of Switzerland. At the same time in England, William Smith was also studying Jurassic-age rocks and noted their repeatable sequences of rock layers and the fossils they contain. In 1799 he published his *law of faunal assemblages,* which explains how groups of sedimentary rock layers can be recognized over wide areas by the unique assemblages of fossils they contain.

During Jurassic time the equator cut across southern Mexico; subduction offshore from western North America formed a deep-ocean trench, with active volcanoes influencing the sediments being deposited around the San Diego area (Figure 2.1).

Jurassic Sedimentary Rocks in San Diego

Jurassic sedimentary rocks can be seen along five canyon floors that extend west of Interstate 15, between the Del Dios Highway on the north and Mira Mesa Boulevard on the south (Figure 2.2). In these canyons the observerwill find steeply tilted sedimentary rock layers

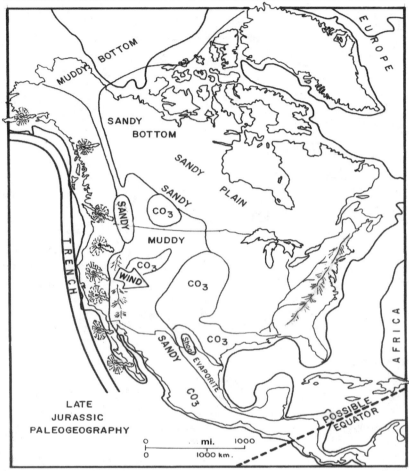

*Figure 2.1. Map of North America during late Jurassic time (about
147 million years ago). The trench lying offshore of western North
America was formed by eastward subduction of the oceanic plate.
The western edge of the continent had a line of volcanoes* 🌿
*running from Alaska to Mexico. The middle of the continent was
flooded by shallow marine water that received various types of
sediments ranging from sands to fossil-rich carbonates (CO_3),
with evaporation producing some salt deposits.*

composed of slightly metamorphosed, dark gray mudstones interbedded with sandstone and conglomerate beds. (For a more detailed view of this area, see the geologic maps of the Del Mar and La Jolla quadrangles by Mike Kennedy in Kennedy and Peterson, 1975.) The rock exposures in the five canyons are similar in appearance though different in detail. The layers of rock are not physically continuous from one canyon to the next, and their differences in composition prevent detailed correlation. These strata were dated after Perry Crampton discovered marine clam fossils

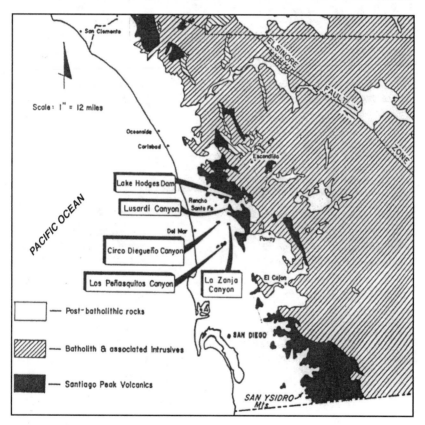

Figure 2.2. Five canyons in San Diego region exposing Jurassic sedimentary rocks.

(*Buchia piochii*) in some of the sandstone beds (Figure 2.3) (Fife, Minch, and Crampton, 1967). These fossils date from latest Jurassic time, 151–142 million years ago, and are the oldest fossils found in the San Diego urban area—so far.

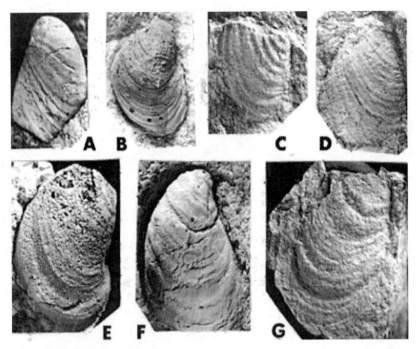

Figure 2.3. Internal molds (fossils) of Buchia piochii *(1.5×) collected in Circo Diegueño Canyon.* Buchia piochii *is a clam of latest Jurassic age. Photographs by Rick Miller.*

The Jurassic sedimentary rock layers contain interesting structures that record their depositional history. For example, currents that transport sediments (such as stream floods and underwater gravity-pulled density currents) deposit them when the energy of the current subsides. The coarsest grains may settle out first followed by progressively finer grains forming a graded bed (Figure 2.4). When successive layers are deposited, the added weight may cause underlying muds to deform, inject upward, and tilt as the sediment layer slides downslope, forming flame structures. We can use sedimentary features such as graded beds and flame structures to determine the bottoms and tops of deformed sedimentary rock layers, that is, to determine which sides were up and which were down at the time the sediment was deposited.

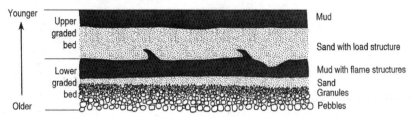

Figure 2.4. Schematic cross section of sedimentary rock layers. Graded beds occur where the coarsest grains lie at the base of a bed, with progressively finer grains lying above them. Flame structures form when mud injects upward into heavier sand and bends, creating "flames" that point downslope. Load structures form when sand sinks into mud.

Remember the law of original horizontality, which tells us that sediments are originally deposited in near-horizontal layers? The San Diego Jurassic strata are no longer horizontal but are now steeply inclined, testifying to ancient compressive forces. What's more, in some canyons the graded beds and flame structures indicate that the strata have been overturned. In Lusardi Creek canyon (near Rancho Santa Fe), for example, the rock layers have been pushed over and now dip 45 degrees to the east, which means that rock layers that were once horizontal have rotated 135 degrees (Figure 2.5). Those were some compressive forces!

NAME OF JURASSIC STRATA

Geologists use the term *formation* for bodies of rock occurring over an area large enough to be shown on a geologic map with a scale of 1:24,000 (1 inch = 2,000 feet). Formations usually take their names from geographic locales where they are particularly well exposed.

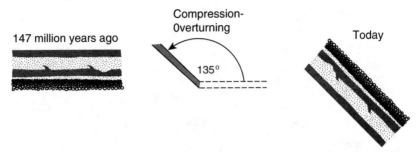

Figure 2.5. Cross sections showing overturning of once-horizontal sedimentary beds.

The Jurassic strata in San Diego are mostly composed of sediments derived from erosion of volcanic rocks, and they have long been assigned the name Santiago Peak Volcanics (named for Santiago Peak in the Santa Ana Mountains of Orange County). But recent radiometric-age analyses by Dave Kimbrough and Chuck Herzig at SDSU indicate that the Santiago Peak Volcanics were formed 128–117 million years ago, making them early Cretaceous instead of Jurassic in age. This means that the Jurassic strata in San Diego are older than the Santiago Peak Volcanics and therefore need a different name to distinguish them from the Santiago Peak Volcanics. They might be assignable to the Bedford Canyon Formation, which underlies the Santiago Peak Volcanics in the Santa Ana Mountains in Orange County, or they could be given a new name. If geologists decide to assign them to a new formation, it should likely refer to the rock exposures in Los Peñasquitos Canyon between Interstates 805 and 15; this area would make a good reference or type section because it lies in a protected City of San Diego park (the other four canyon localities are all private property and may be altered or destroyed by future development).

COMPOSITION OF JURASSIC SEDIMENTARY ROCKS
To better understand the composition of San Diego's Jurassic sedimentary rocks, Duane Balch examined thin-section samples of Jurassic sandstones under a microscope and found that the sand grains, on average, are small pieces of volcanic rock (47%), plagioclase feld-

spar (47%), volcanic quartz (5%), and potassium feldspar (1%). The sand grains were derived almost totally from volcanic sources, with little or no continental debris evident, suggesting that the sediments came from erosion of volcanic islands rising out of the sea (Balch, Bartling, and Abbott, 1984).

The sand-sized volcanic-rock fragments are intermediate in composition, meaning that their composition lies between magmas that intrude up through the oceanic crust and flow onto the ocean floor and magmas that move up through the continental crust and then flow out onto continents. The plagioclase feldspar mineral found in the volcanic-rock fragments is mostly andesine, a sodium-rich variety common in volcanic rocks of intermediate composition. When viewed under a microscope, the rare sand grains of quartz are water clear, have symmetric crystal shapes indicating a high-temperature origin, and have water-filled inclusions—features that are typical of quartz formed in volcanic igneous rocks. In contrast, common quartz derived from plutonic igneous rocks is asymmetrical, somewhat cloudy, may have mineral inclusions, and a single grain is commonly made of multiple crystals. Common quartz is usually the most abundant grain type found in any sandstone, yet it is absent in the Jurassic strata found in San Diego, providing further evidence that the sources of these volcanic-rock sediments were in the ocean and were not part of the continent.

As sand grains roll along during transportation (such as in a stream), grain-to-grain abrasion smooths and rounds their exterior surfaces. The sand grains found in the Jurassic sandstones in San Diego, however, have very angular exteriors, indicating that they did not travel far and were deposited near their volcanic source rocks.

By integrating all the preceding evidence we come up with a picture of a late Jurassic line of oceanic volcanoes with intermediate composition magmas. On the sides of the volcanoes facing westward away from the continent, gravity-induced slope failures carried sands and gravels downslope into deeper ocean waters where the sediments accumulated in basins on the volcano slopes. Remains of latest Jurassic marine organisms were buried in these sediments. The entire sedimentary pile was later deformed and folded, and some areas were overturned during collision of the sea floor with the continental landmass. The older oceanic sediments were then added to the growing continental edge in the deformed positions we find them today.

Jurassic Field Trip: Los Peñasquitos Canyon

A long walk along the floor of Los Peñasquitos Canyon (Figure 2.6) reveals the intriguing Jurassic sedimentary strata. After parking at the eastern end of the Los Peñasquitos Canyon Reserve off Black

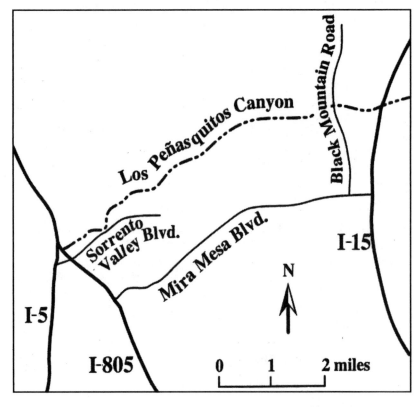

Figure 2.6. Map for Los Peñasquitos Canyon field trip.

Mountain Road (*Thomas Guide,* p. 1189, D7),* a downstream walk of 2.8 miles (4.5 km) will bring you to the lowest (oldest) exposed Jurassic strata at some impressive, but seasonal, waterfalls (Figure 2.7). Alternatively, you can park at the canyon mouth in Sorrento Valley (*Thomas Guide,* p. 1208, C5) and walk upstream 1.4 miles (2.3 km) to the top of the Jurassic strata; the trip from the canyon mouth in Sorrento Valley to the waterfalls is 2.8 miles (4.5 km).

Figure 2.7. Waterfalls over late Jurassic, dipping sedimentary rocks in Los Peñasquitos Canyon.

The strata you will encounter are dipping 48 degrees toward the west. In a nonoverturned sequence of sedimentary rock layers, the lower strata are older than the upper strata deposited on top of

*Thomas Guide refers to *The Thomas Guide to San Diego County* published by Thomas Bros. Maps & Books; it is available in most bookstores and supermarkets. Even though the *Thomas Guide* is updated annually, the map coordinates remain the same from year to year.

them (law of superposition). In Los Peñasquitos Canyon, due to the steep westward tilt of the strata, the lowest (oldest) rocks are encountered upstream at higher elevations. As you walk downstream, you "climb up" the sedimentary section through progressively younger rock layers. One of the great joys of geology is the three-dimensional thinking it requires. Study the cross section in Figure 2.8 and use 3D thinking while you are in the canyon. Expand your mind and enjoy visualizing how you can walk *downhill* and, at the same time, *climb up* the sedimentary section.

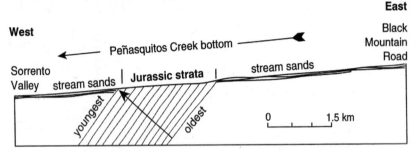

Figure 2.8. Schematic cross section of dipping Jurassic strata in Los Peñasquitos Canyon.

FIELD OBSERVATIONS

At the waterfall region at the base of the Jurassic sedimentary rock sequence, notice the thick beds of granule- to boulder-sized conglomerate containing angular pieces of volcanic rocks (Figure 2.9). A conglomerate containing angular pieces of rock is commonly called a *breccia*. Also notice the chunks of volcanic conglomerate/sandstone that were ripped up (eroded) and incorporated into the sedimentary masses as they moved down the submerged slopes of ancient volcanoes. Submarine landslides and gravity-pulled debris flows eroded the sloping sea floor they moved across. If you look carefully you can see rare belemnite fossils (the white calcite skeletal cones that formed part of the internal skeletons of the extinct squid-like *Cylindroteuthis*).

While in the canyon, look carefully to see the following features in the Jurassic sedimentary rocks:

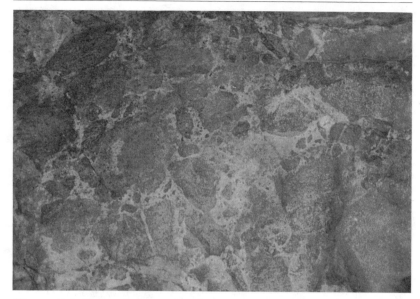

Figure 2.9. Volcanic-clast conglomerate at upper waterfall in Los Peñasquitos Canyon.

- Graded beds (Figure 2.4): Find a sandstone bed displaying grain sizes grading from coarse at the bottom to finer near the top. This is evidence of deposition from a gravity-powered, subsea, short-lived turbid flow of sediment.
- Mudstone caps: Notice the layers of very fine-grained gray mud that settled from suspension and were deposited on top of the sand layers.
- Load structures (Figure 2.4): Look for a sand layer that sank into an underlying mud layer after it was deposited as a heavy load on top of the weak sea-floor muds.
- Flame structures (Figure 2.4): Look for mud that squirted up into overlying heavy sands and deformed (pointed) downslope.
- Rip-up clasts: Note the gravel-sized pieces (*clasts*) of dark mud that were eroded off the sea floor by passing debris flows and density currents and incorporated into sandstone and conglomerate beds.

- Trace fossils: Look for cylindrical, tube-like burrows left in muds by small invertebrate animals as they traveled across, rested in, and ate the organic-rich muds.

Jurassic Depositional Environment

The overall changes in grain size within the Jurassic sedimentary section tell of changes in the depositional environment through time. Coarse gravels and sands accumulated in submarine channels that received high-energy debris flows; graded sands were deposited in sedimentary lobes built outward from channels. At times when channels migrated to other areas, thick intervals of mud slowly settled from suspension in seawater during these quiet-water conditions.

Further collecting efforts in the Jurassic rocks have led to the discovery of other fossils in addition to the clam *Buchia piochii* and belemnites (*Cylindroteuthis sp.*). Some fossils have been discovered through microscopic examination of thinly sliced pieces of mudstone. These fossils include oyster-shell fragments, echinoid (sea urchin) spines, sponge spicules (needle-like skeletal pieces), and radiolaria (zooplankton). All of these fossils verify that the ancient sediments accumulated in a marine environment.

The dominant rock type is mudstone made of dark gray clay plus silt derived by weathering and erosion of volcanic rock sources. The mudstones contain fossil burrows and tracks of animals (*Zoophycos* and *Nereites*) that suggest deeper marine water. At this time in the region the sea was lapping up against a volcanic massif. The generally quiet marine environment was interrupted occasionally as gravity-pulled masses of sand and gravel flowed down the submarine slope into deeper water. Sarah Hosken-Bartling showed that the submarine gravity flows moved toward the southwest and were deposited in the sedimentary rock layers we see today.

CHAPTER 3
CRETACEOUS HISTORY

Cretaceous time is defined as having occurred from 142 to 65 million years ago (Figure 1.5). Rocks of Cretaceous age are common throughout Europe. These rocks and fossils were studied in different countries; in 1822, Jean-Baptiste-Julien d'Omalius d'Halloy tied the studies together and defined the *Terrain Cretace* with a type section in the Paris basin of France and adjacent parts of Belgium and the Netherlands.

In San Diego, Cretaceous rocks are important recorders of history. During this time the greatest volume of magma rose and cooled to form the plutonic rocks now exposed in the Peninsular Ranges. These ranges include many familiar mountains, such as the Lagunas, the Cuyamacas, the Santa Anas, and Mount Palomar. Sediments eroding off those once high-standing mountains were mostly carried westward and dumped into the ocean. Locally, Cretaceous rocks are best exposed in La Jolla, Bird Rock, and Point Loma.

Cretaceous Sedimentary Rocks in San Diego

During most of Cretaceous time in San Diego, the eastward-moving oceanic plate was rapidly subducting beneath the western edge of North America. Melting of subducted crustal material produced massive volumes of magma that intruded upward and cooled below

31

the surface (Figure 3.1). The subduction process generated heat as well as tapped into the super hot asthenosphere to yield great volumes of magma and create a high and large mountain mass. Today this material is seen as the plutonic igneous rocks of the Peninsular Ranges. Erosion of mountains yields large volumes of sediment that are transported downslope and deposited in low-lying basins. In the San Diego area, no sedimentary rocks have been found that accumulated during early Cretaceous time (142–99 million years ago); Cretaceous sedimentary rocks found here represent only part of late Cretaceous time (99–65 million years ago). The lack of early Cretaceous sedimentary rocks is probably due to (1) the high topography and lack of basins to catch and hold the sediment, (2) later erosion that removed sedimentary rock, and (3) major faults moving huge areas of rock northward out of the area.

What is the geologic fate of a mountain range? Huge mountain masses interfere with atmospheric circulation, causing rain and snow to fall. The downhill flow of streams wears down landmasses, transporting and dumping the sedimentary debris into the oceans. Near the middle of Cretaceous time, about 95 million years ago, our backcountry mountains presumably were at their maximum height due to rapid subduction of the steeply dipping oceanic plate (called the Farallon plate), resulting in the intrusion of tremendous volumes of magma that crystallized to form the La Posta plutonic rock body that dominates much of the eastern Peninsular Ranges. By late Cretaceous time, erosion had eaten significantly into the mountains, stripping off much of the overlying metamorphic and volcanic rock cover and exposing the once deeply buried plutonic rocks; in the process, large volumes of sediment were produced. But why, then, do we find only a relatively small volume of Cretaceous sedimentary rock in San Diego today? Sediments accumulate in topographically low places—some accumulate in lakes and stream valleys, but most are eventually dumped into ocean basins. In the San Diego region during early and middle Cretaceous time, the massive mountains probably forced the shoreline far to the west of where it is today; consequently, sediments were deposited in ocean basins farther west beyond those ancient shorelines. Later faulting probably moved much of the sediments northward out of the area.

LATE CRETACEOUS
(95 Ma)

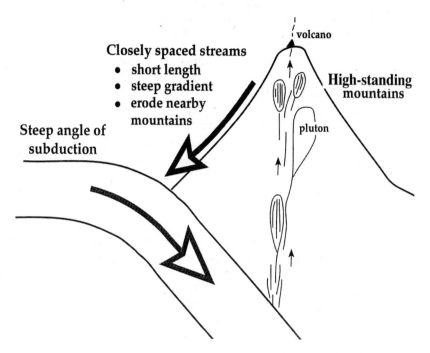

Figure 3.1. *Exaggerated west-to-east cross section through the San Diego area about 95 million years ago (Ma). The subducting oceanic plate generated large volumes of magma; some reached the surface as volcanoes, but most cooled underground as plutons. Short, steep streams eroded the mountains, dumping coarse sediment at the base of the mountains and into the ocean.*

Cretaceous Formations

A nonmarine sedimentary mass of late Cretaceous age was named the Lusardi Formation by Chuck Nordstrom. The formation is exposed at inland sites in Poway, Rancho Santa Fe, Carlsbad, and Alpine. These nonmarine sedimentary rock layers are overlain in western outcrops by marine sedimentary rocks. In 1971 Mike Kennedy and George Moore subdivided the marine sedimentary rocks of late Cretaceous age into two formations. The lower portion dominated by mudstone and sandstone was named the Point Loma Formation, and the upper portion overlying it, composed of conglomerate and sandstone, was named the Cabrillo Formation. Both of these marine formations derive their names from the southern tip of Point Loma in Cabrillo National Monument.

CRETACEOUS NONMARINE STRATA

The oldest of the Cretaceous sedimentary rocks found in San Diego were deposited as an apron of coarse sedimentary debris eroded off the ancestral Peninsular Ranges and deposited along their western slopes. The sediments accumulated about 90 to 75 million years ago in alluvial fans (fan-shaped aprons of sediment at the base of mountain slopes) and within stream valleys. These deposits, known as the Lusardi Formation, take their name from exposures near the mouth of Lusardi Creek where it joins the San Dieguito River near Rancho Santa Fe. Other prominent areas of outcrop occur near Carlsbad, Poway, San Vicente Reservoir, and Alpine. The most readily accessible outcrops are boulder-rich muddy sandstones exposed in roadcuts along Poway Road as it rises eastward from Poway toward Highway 67 (Figure 5.14). (These outcrops can be located on the geologic map of the Poway quadrangle in Kennedy and Peterson, 1975.)

The Lusardi Formation is mostly a poorly sorted, cobble-to-boulder conglomerate consisting of debris derived locally from the nearby plutonic, volcanic, and metamorphic basement rocks. Some individual boulders are larger than 30 feet (10 m) in diameter. These coarse boulder-bearing sediments lie on top of an erosion surface that formed during late Cretaceous time. This now-buried surface was an ancient landscape of hilly topography containing many hundreds of feet of relief (shown as sub-Lusardi Formation unconformity in Figure 3.2). Erosion formed this ancient surface and removed a large volume of the underlying sediments. While the sediments of the Lusardi Formation were exposed at the Cretaceous surface, they were subjected to severe and deep weathering. This weathering caused much in-place decomposition of rock and the development of thick soils. (The general formation of ancient soils is discussed in Chapter 4.)

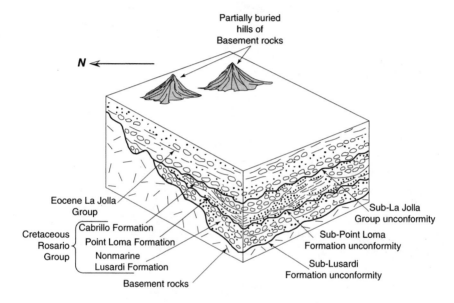

Figure 3.2. Schematic diagram of Cretaceous and Eocene rock bodies in San Diego. Plutonic and volcanic basement rocks were severely eroded and then mostly covered by sediments deposited in late Cretaceous and Eocene time. Some bedrock hilltops, such as Cowles and Black mountains, stand above the sedimentary rocks. Each unconformity represents an old land surface that was later buried by younger sediments. Adapted from Peterson and Nordstrom, 1970.

CRETACEOUS MARINE STRATA

In San Diego, around 85 million years ago, the underlying magma supply feeding the volcanoes and deep plutonic masses of the Peninsular Ranges was cut off as the oceanic Farallon plate began shallowing its angle of subduction beneath western North America. This change in tectonic style caused the sites of magma intrusion to move eastward below Arizona and New Mexico. Meanwhile, the agents of erosion, mainly running water and gravity, continued to eat into the local mountains from above. As the San Diego landmass was eroding on top and being reduced in size, it was also cooling at plutonic depths and contracting. The combined effects of erosion at the surface and cooling at depth caused the landmass to shrink and sink enough to allow the seashore to advance eastward into the San Diego area.

Marine sediments and fossils deposited during late Cretaceous time are well exposed in the sea cliffs at Point Loma and La Jolla (Figure 3.3) as well as in roadcuts in Carlsbad. The west side of the Point Loma peninsula between the U.S. Coast Guard lighthouse and Ocean Beach offers spectacular sea-cliff exposures of Cretaceous rocks. Access to the beach is limited along this stretch of coastline but is available at the tidepools of Cabrillo National Monument, below the end of Ladera Street along Sunset Cliffs, and at several of the coves along Sunset Cliffs and Ocean Beach. In the La Jolla area Cretaceous marine sandstones and mudstones occur from False Point on the south all the way north through Bird Rock, Windansea, La Jolla Cove, and around La Jolla Bay to the La Jolla Beach and Tennis Club. At inland Carlsbad, these sedimentary rocks are exposed in roadcuts along El Camino Real north of Faraday Avenue and along College Boulevard between El Camino Real and Faraday Avenue. All these rocks are part of the Point Loma Formation, except for the rocks in the stretch between False Point and Bird Rock, which are part of the Cabrillo Formation.

Lying on top of the Point Loma Formation are the marine strata of the Cabrillo Formation; these strata contain large volumes of cobble and boulder conglomerate. The conglomerate clasts are pieces of the Peninsular Ranges plutons, Santiago Peak Volcanics, Julian Schist, and numerous volcanic-rock clasts that probably came from

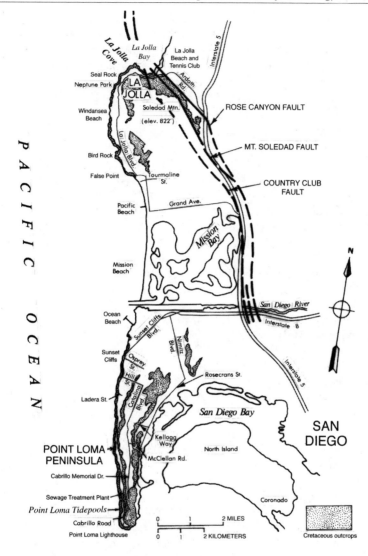

Figure 3.3. Map of San Diego west of the Rose Canyon fault zone, from Point Loma to La Jolla Bay. Note the locations of marine Cretaceous sedimentary rocks.

volcanoes that once were built on top of the Cretaceous Peninsular Ranges. In other words, the conglomerate clasts are preserved pieces of the Cretaceous mountains. These conglomerates are exposed in roadcuts along Cabrillo Road in southern Point Loma heading down to the tidepools and in the cutbank behind the sewage treatment plant. The sea cliffs between northernmost Pacific Beach (False Point) and Bird Rock also offer excellent exposures of Cabrillo conglomerate.

Sea levels have risen and fallen during Earth's history, and one of the intervals of highest sea levels occurred during middle Cretaceous time (about 120–90 million years ago). During this time the interior of North America was flooded by seawater as the Gulf of Mexico and the Arctic Ocean connected into one seaway, splitting the continent into two separate landmasses. Yet even during this global highstand of sea level, the huge volcanic/plutonic mass of the ancestral Peninsular Ranges kept the San Diego region well above the water. It was not until erosion reduced the size of the San Diego landmass that the seas could impinge on the mountain front.

DETERMINING THE CRETACEOUS AGE

To understand the late Cretaceous history of the San Diego region, we must inspect the geologic record from that time. We do this by examining the fossils and interpreting the sedimentary rocks containing them. The sedimentary rocks and their contained fossils found in the sea cliffs west of the Rose Canyon fault zone give us our best materials to study (Figure 3.3). The Rose Canyon fault zone is a typical California fault; it is aligned north-northwest to south-southeast, and its western side is moving toward the north. South of Ardath Road the fault zone takes a slight westerly bend, which causes the western block to push northward against the bend, thereby compressing and folding the sedimentary strata. This activity is responsible for the uplifting of Mount Soledad and the down-warping of Mission Bay (Figure 3.4). The folding of the rock layers lifted them above sea level, allowing us to get a good look at them today. The Rose Canyon fault zone remains active, and the compressional folding of the land continues.

How do we read a sequence of sedimentary rocks such as this? The investigation begins by examining the oldest rocks exposed at

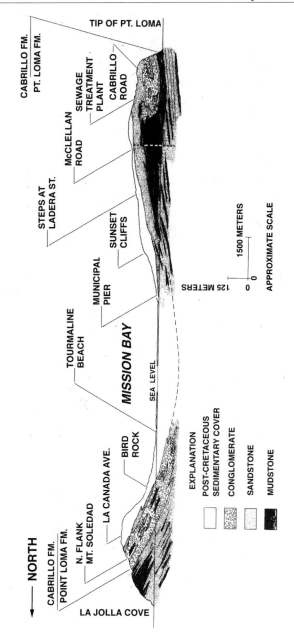

Figure 3.4. North–south cross section through marine sedimentary rocks west of the Rose Canyon fault zone. Modified from drawing by Eli Zlotnik.

the base of the sedimentary rock sequence; we then proceed up-section, reading each layer "up through time" to understand the record of past events and to reconstruct the ancient world. For example, one could traverse geologic time in San Diego by beginning with the dipping sandstone beds in the sea cliffs just south of the La Jolla Beach and Tennis Club (Figure 3.3), and then walking south-west along the mudstone cliffs surrounding La Jolla Bay. Keep traveling westerly across sandstone beds around La Jolla Cove, on southward beyond Bird Rock, and finally past cliffs of conglomerate around False Point. This north-to-south traverse will carry you upward through geologic time; a careful examination of the sedimentary rocks will reveal evidence of ancient sedimentation and erosion as well as the remains and tracks of extinct marine organisms. From this evidence we can reconstruct the ancient world.

How can we determine the ages of the sedimentary rocks at La Jolla and Point Loma? We do this by collecting and identifying fossils and placing them into their positions in the worldwide sequence of fossils. Bill Sliter did this for the foraminifera (single-celled protozoans with calcareous shells that are readily preserved as fossils) as part of his Ph.D. dissertation; Dave Bukry examined a type of nannofossil known as coccoliths (calcite platelets secreted by single-celled yellow-green algae), and Will Elder updated the classification of the ammonites (shelled molluscs similar to the modern-day *Nautilus*). These three distinct groups of fossils all correlate decisively with fossil assemblages found in rocks of Cretaceous age worldwide. The Point Loma Formation fossils correlate with the upper Campanian Series established by H. Coquand in 1857 in the Champagne region of France (the upper Campanian occurred 76–71 million years ago). The conglomeratic Cabrillo Formation does not have as rich a fossil assemblage as the Point Loma Formation, but we estimate that it is still within the Campanian age.

Magnetic polarity data in the mudstone cliffs around La Jolla Bay identify an interval of south magnetic polarity interpreted to be the reversed polarity interval called Chron 32R2 (Figure 3.5). Comparing the fossil and magnetic data from the Point Loma Formation to the worldwide standards, where radiometric ages are known, yields ages for the Point Loma and Cabrillo Formations ranging from about 76 to 72 million years old.

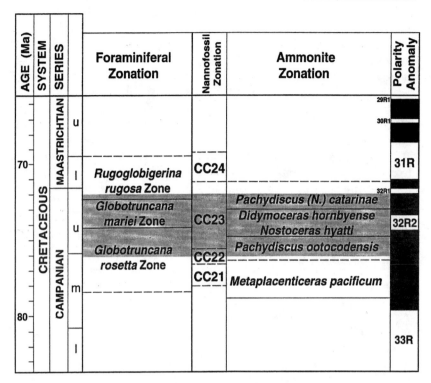

Figure 3.5. Age of the Point Loma Formation (shaded interval) in millions of years (Ma) as determined from fossils and the magnetic polarity-reversal time scale. In the figure, times when Earth's magnetic pole pointed north are shown in black whereas south polarities (R = reversed) are white. (cc = coccolith, the remains of certain yellow-green algae; u = upper; m = middle; l = lower.) "System" and "Series" are biostratigraphic equivalents of "Period" and "Epoch" which are rock stratigraphic terms.

CRETACEOUS DEPOSITIONAL ENVIRONMENTS

The Cretaceous rock layers from La Jolla Bay to northern Pacific Beach lead upward through about 4 million years of geologic time. They tell an interesting story that Bill Bartling and I interpret as beginning with shallow marine water about 3 feet (1 m) deep that rapidly deepened to about 0.62 mile (1 km) in depth (Bartling and Abbott, 1983). The lowered sea floor received large volumes of sediment that poured into the deep water and accumulated on the sea floor.

The rapid deepening of seawater was probably caused by a late Cretaceous fault that ran north-northwest through San Diego, separating the deep basin of Point Loma and La Jolla on its west side from the shallow-water marine shelf on its east side. Some sedimentary deposits on the Cretaceous marine shelf are now found in the vicinity of Palomar Airport in Carlsbad. The suspected Cretaceous fault is long extinct and lies buried beneath younger sedimentary rocks, making it hard to prove its existence.

What happened in the deep basin in the La Jolla and Point Loma area? Tor Nilsen and I recognized a submarine fan (the oceanic analogue of an alluvial fan) that built its way westward and slowly began filling the marine basin with sediments derived from the erosion of the ancestral Peninsular Ranges (Figure 3.6) (Nilsen and Abbott, 1981).

How does a submarine fan form? It forms in much the same way that an alluvial fan forms on land. In each case a massive apron of sediment accumulates at the base of a steep slope; the apron is composed of fan-shaped masses, each fed by a sediment-filled channel. The big difference for submarine fans is that the whole sedimentary system is under water. The sediment-transport mechanisms in submarine fans are mostly dense flows of sand and mud pulled downslope by gravity, with internal water carried along for the ride. On land, in alluvial fans, gravity-pulled debris flows occur high on the fan, but most of the downward transport of sediment occurs from running water, which flows, erodes, and transports sediments in its familiar way. In the ocean, coarse sediments (sand and gravel) brought to the ocean by rivers tend to gather near the shoreline until they build up into large enough masses to be pulled downslope by gravity, while fine-grained mud (clay and fine silt) floats out into deeper water where it slowly settles to the deep-sea floor under the pull of gravity. A submarine fan has a gravel-filled inner-fan valley near its landward apex (Figure 3.6). The inner-fan valley

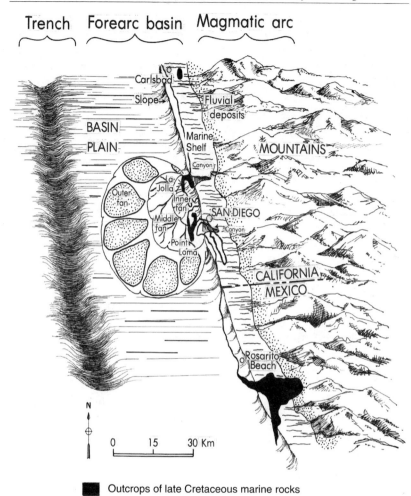

Trench Forearc basin Magmatic arc

Carlsbad
Slope
BASIN
PLAIN
Fluvial deposits
Marine Shelf
Canyon
MOUNTAINS
La Jolla
Outer fan
Inner fan
Middle fan
SAN DIEGO
Canyon
Point Loma
CALIFORNIA
MEXICO
Rosarito Beach

N

0   15   30 Km

■ Outcrops of late Cretaceous marine rocks

Figure 3.6. Paleogeographic map of San Diego in late Cretaceous time. The steep submarine escarpment separating the marine shelf from the basin plain was probably caused by a fault. Modified from Nilsen and Abbott, 1981.

opens out into a radiating pattern of sand-filled channels that characterize the middle fan region. At the mouths of the channels, finer sediments pour out onto the outer fan, with some of the clays continuing to travel in suspension out onto the basin plain. With time, the submarine fan grows seaward, building its way outward and upward.

To better understand this process, refer to Figure 3.6 and then employ geologic thinking, including the fourth dimension (time): Visualize mud being deposited on the basin plain, alternating mud and sand layers accumulating in the outer fan area, sand being deposited in the middle fan, and gravel accumulating in the inner fan. Notice that the finer sediments are farther offshore and in deeper water, whereas the coarser sediments are closer to shore and in shallower water. Now visualize the whole submarine fan system operating over time as more sediments are brought by rivers to the shoreline. The submarine fan builds outward (*progrades*) to the west and begins filling the marine basin with ever-coarser sediments, yielding a vertical sequence of sedimentary rocks whose sediment sizes, in general, coarsen upward (Figure 3.7). In this way, the fine muds of the basin-plain are buried, first beneath the muds and sands of the outer fan, then by the sands of the middle fan, and later by gravels deposited in the inner-fan valley as the entire submarine fan grows and progrades westward. Try sketching these three-dimensional relationships on paper, in a time sequence, in order to better understand the process of submarine fan growth. This exercise will help prepare you for the field trips to be described.

Paleontology

Cretaceous-age sedimentary rocks in San Diego County contain well-preserved and abundant fossils. These fossils represent fauna and flora that lived in a climate that was more tropical than the present climate in San Diego. Groves of dawn redwood trees dotted the upland regions, some of the earliest flowering plants occupied the lower coastal slopes, and plant-eating duck-billed and armored dinosaurs inhabited the coastal plain. Offshore, exotic species of clams and snails lived on and in the soft muddy sea floor, coiled and straight squid-like ammonites jetted about in the water column

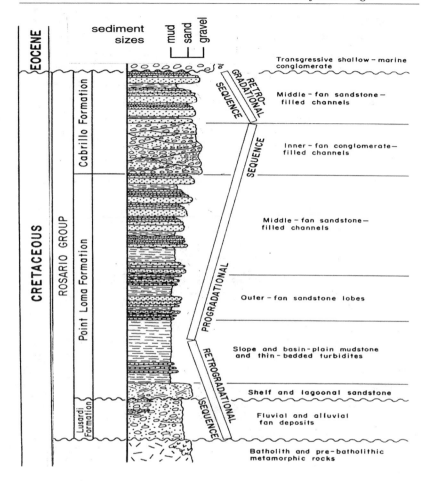

Figure 3.7. Generalized vertical section through the Cretaceous sedimentary rocks of San Diego. Progradation, *marked by an interval of coarsening-upward sediments, occurs when sediment masses build outward and push the shoreline seaward;* retrogradation, *marked by an interval of fining-upward sediments, occurs when rising sea level causes a landward shift of sedimentary environments. See Figure 1.3 for discussion of "mud, sand, gravel." Modified from Nilsen and Abbott, 1981.*

preying on fish, and giant sea-going monitor lizards, called mosa-saurs, hunted both fish and ammonites alike.

Fossils collected from the Point Loma Formation are, for the most part, shelled remains of marine molluscs, such as pelecypods (clams and oysters), gastropods (snails), cephalopods (nautiloids and ammonites), and scaphopods (tusk shells). Other types of marine fossils from these rocks include calcareous plates of microscopic algae (coccolithophores), tiny shells of single-celled foraminifera, delicate shells and claws of decapods (crabs), and thin tests of echinoids (sea urchins). Rare remains of marine vertebrates have also been recovered from the Point Loma Formation; these include shark teeth (*Squalicorax, Squalus,* and *Scaporhyncus*), ratfish or chimaera teeth (holocephalian), bony fish otoliths (earbones of sea catfish, angle-fish, bonefish, butterfly fish, and cusk eel), and mosasaur vertebrae and ribs (extinct giant marine monitor lizards). The Point Loma Formation has also produced sparse remains of land-dwelling organisms, including plants (conifers and angiosperms) and dinosaurs (discussed later).

As noted earlier, the sandstones and mudstones of the Point Loma Formation were deposited in a variety of marine environments ranging from intertidal through the continental shelf to the deeper ocean floor. These various paleoenvironments are represented by distinct types of sedimentary rocks and their contained fossils. Intertidal coarse-grained sandstones exposed in Carlsbad contain fossil remains of sedentary colonial rudistid clams (*Coralliochama orcutti*) (Figure 3.8), armored turban snails (*Xenophora*), and oysters cemented to hard bottom objects (*Ostrea*). Rudistids are a unique group of extinct, reef-building clams that built an enlarged conical lower valve (shell) cemented during life to a hard bottom, and a caplike upper valve. Whole rudistid fossils found in San Diego have heavy and tough shells as tall as 6 inches; they are most commonly found as fragments. Broken shells were readily transported and preserved as pieces of gravel. The armored *Xenophora* snail consists of a low-spiraled shell with rounded pebbles cemented to the outside of the shell. As the xenophorid snail grew, it selected progressively larger pebbles to attach to its enlarging spiraled shell. These interesting snails may be seen by visiting the San Diego Museum of Natural History in Balboa Park.

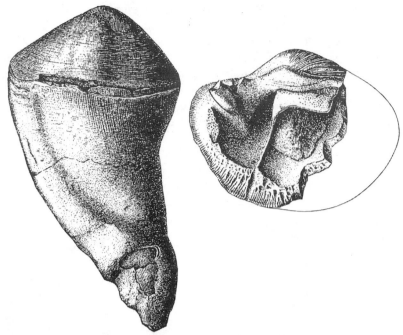

Figure 3.8. Late Cretaceous rudistid clam, Coralliochama orcutti.
(Left) *paired valve showing conical lower valve and cup-shaped
upper valve;* (right) *internal view of upper valve.*

Continental-shelf sandstones and mudstones also are exposed
at Carlsbad. These rocks contain a diverse invertebrate fossil assemblage that includes cowries, winged apporahid snails, moon
snails, rock scallops, pen shells, crassatellid clams, tellinid clams,
coiled and straight ammonites, coiled nautiloids, predaceous crabs,
and burrowing heart urchins. Locally, the mudstones contain pockets of concentrated fossils. Some pockets consist of a single, large
ammonite shell covered on one side with the attached shells of rock
scallops, oysters, and calcareous worm tubes. Such fossil concentrations represent small patch reefs that formed on the sea floor
when opportunistic encrusting species colonized the shell of a dead
ammonite. Apparently these shells, and sometimes dinosaur bones,

were the only available hard substrates invertebrate organisms could attach to on the soft muddy Cretaceous sea floor.

Cretaceous marine rocks exposed in the sea cliffs between La Jolla Shores and La Jolla Cove consist of a thick sequence (825+ feet [250+ m]) of shallow-marine sandstone overlain by deep-water mudstone that grades upward to deep-marine sandstone (Figure 3.7). The shallow-marine sandstones just south of La Jolla Shores contain broken shells of rudistid clams (*Coralliochama orcutti*), rock scallops (*Spondylus*), and brachiopods (*Megeria*). Fossils in the over-lying deep-water mudstones include straight ammonites (*Baculites*), coiled ammonites (*Pachydiscus*) (Figure 3.9), large thin-shelled clams (*Inoceramus*) (Figure 3.10), and transported rudistid clams (*Coralliochama*).

Figure 3.9 (left). Late Cretaceous ammonite, Pachydiscus catari-nae *(black bar in upper-right corner of photograph is 0.4 inch [1 cm] long).*

Figure 3.10 (right). Large clam, Inoceramus n. sp. *(approx. 0.5x), found in Cretaceous marine rock at La Jolla Bay.*

AMMONITES

Worldwide, ammonites are probably the most characteristic marine fossils of Cretaceous-age rocks. These delicately chambered molluscs are extinct cousins of the modern-day *Nautilus* (Figure 3.11), a predaceous free-swimming squid-like animal that survives today in the deep water of the southwestern Pacific Ocean and Indian Ocean. Most ammonites were spirally coiled in a vertical plane, though some were straight. Ammonites evolved in Paleozoic time more than 360 million years ago and became extinct at the end of Mesozoic time, 65 million years ago. Because evolutionary rates were relatively rapid in ammonites, the various genera and species serve as guides for estimating the age of the rocks containing them.

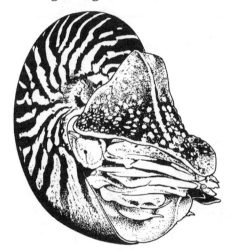

Figure 3.11. Modern-day Nautilus. *Live specimens may be seen in some large aquariums.*

The ammonites found in the Point Loma Formation include at least four different species characteristic of late Cretaceous time. These 76–72-million-year-old ammonites consist of the straight species *Baculites lomaensis* and the coiled species *Pachydiscus caterinae, Anapachydiscus peninsularis*, and *Neophylloceras ramosum*. *Pachydiscus caterinae* is rather common in the fossil beds at Carlsbad, with some specimens reaching 3+ feet (1+ m) in diameter.

If we examine closely the shell of *P. caterinae,* we find that it is made up of an inner region (the phragmacone) of small regularly spaced chambers and an outer region (the body chamber) with a single large terminal chamber housing the animal's body (Figure 3.12). Internally, individual chambers are separated by delicately folded walls, called septa. The chambers are connected to one another by a crystalline tube, a siphuncle, that is used to pump in or remove gas from the inner chambers, allowing the animal to rise or sink like a submarine. Where the septum meets the outside of the shell, a fernlike pattern is produced (Figure 3.9). This suture pat-

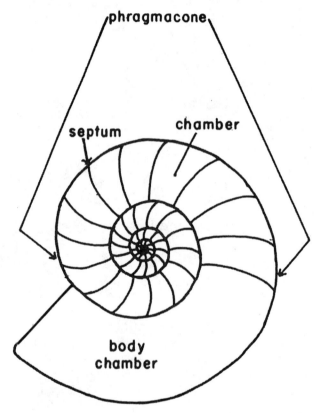

Figure 3.12. Internal structure of an ammonoid shell.

tern, as it is called, is characteristic for each group of ammonites and is useful in identifying and classifying individual species.

Although all ammonites are extinct, their evolutionary cousin, the chambered *Nautilus*, serves as a good model of how ammonites lived. The *Nautilus* is a predator on fish and crustaceans and also is an active scavenger. It swims backwards using a jet of water expelled from its body. *Nautilus* can regulate its buoyancy, and therefore its vertical position in the water column, by secreting metabolic gases that are distributed through the siphuncle to the inner chambers. Rising up and down like a submarine in a daily cycle and swimming in pursuit of prey, the *Nautilus* has been a successful inhabitant of the world's ocean for millions of years.

FORAMINIFERA

Foraminifera, or forams as they are informally called, are microscopic, single-celled, amoeba-like protozoans that live in marine environments ranging from nearshore to abyssal water depths. Most forams live on or in sea-floor sediments and are called benthonic or benthic forams. Other forams have evolved to inhabit open-water environments near the ocean surface and are called planktonic or planktic forams. Forams secrete a hard calcareous shell around or within their protoplasm. These shells can be very common as microfossils in ancient sea-floor sediments.

Micropaleontologists who study the fossil record of foraminifera have used the delicate morphology of these tiny shells to identify thousands of species of extinct forams; they have documented a long evolutionary history for this group of diminutive organisms. Planktonic forams, because of their wide oceanic distribution and rapid rates of evolution, are useful in dating ancient sedimentary rocks. Benthonic forams, although not as useful in determining geologic ages, are useful indicators of ancient sea-floor conditions such as water depth, temperature, and sediment type.

Local Cretaceous foram assemblages include at least 150 species from Carlsbad, 225 species from La Jolla, and 155 species from Point Loma. The Carlsbad assemblage is dominated by shallow-water benthonic species that lived on the ancient continental shelf. The assemblages from La Jolla and Point Loma contain more planktonic species and document bathyal conditions with water depths of about 3,000 feet. This deep-water foram assemblage also contains shells of shallow-water species that were transported into deeper water by turbidity currents.

DINOSAURS OF SAN DIEGO COUNTY

Although dinosaur bones are not common in California, five discoveries have been made in San Diego County—one in La Jolla, one in Sunset Cliffs, and three in Carlsbad. All of the San Diego dinosaur fossils have been found in the Point Loma Formation, and all were found by Brad Riney of the San Diego Museum of Natural History. Rocks bearing dinosaur bones in San Diego are generally of the same age as the famous dinosaur-bearing rocks of the Red Deer River region in southern Alberta, Canada. Whereas the remains of many different species of dinosaurs have been found and described in that region, only two kinds of dinosaurs are presently known to have lived in the San Diego area. These dinosaurs include an indeterminate species of hadrosaur (duck-billed dinosaur) thought to be closely related to *Lambeosaurus* or *Saurolophus* and an indeterminate species of nodosaur (armored dinosaur) probably closely related to *Panaplosaurus*. The hadrosaur fossil material consists of an incomplete back vertebra collected in 1967 from the sea cliffs of La Jolla Bay, a femur collected in 1983 and a series of 13 tail vertebrae collected in 1986 from a construction site near Palomar Airport in Carlsbad, and a fragment of a lower jaw collected in 1989 from a beach cobble found along Sunset Cliffs.

The nodosaur fossil material was collected in Carlsbad in 1987. It consists of a partial skeleton, including pelvic bones, back legs, incomplete front legs, ribs, dermal bony armor, and teeth (Figure 3.13). The Carlsbad nodosaur probably approached 13 feet (4 m) in length and in life was covered by a dense armor of bone actually forming in the skin (Figure 3.14). This dermal armor consisted of thick shoulder patches, low-keeled spinal plates, and an interlocking mosaic of polygonal pelvic ossicles. The teeth of nodosaurs indicate that they were plant eaters related to the familiar club-tailed ankylosaurs and distantly related to *Stegosaurus*, with its large dorsal plates and tail spikes. The Carlsbad specimen is the first

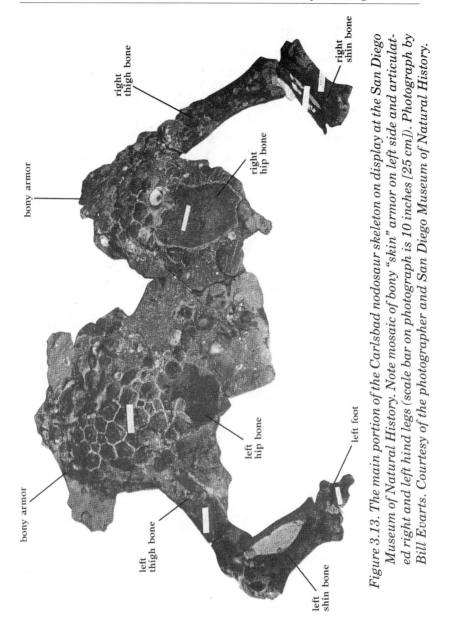

Figure 3.13. The main portion of the Carlsbad nodosaur skeleton on display at the San Diego Museum of Natural History. Note mosaic of bony "skin" armor on left side and articulated right and left hind legs (scale bar on photograph is 10 inches [25 cm]). Photograph by Bill Evarts. Courtesy of the photographer and San Diego Museum of Natural History.

record of a nodosaur in California. Take a visit to the San Diego Museum of Natural History in Balboa Park and have a close look at this dinosaur skeleton.

Why are dinosaur remains so rare in California? They are rare because the sedimentary rocks in California of the right age to contain their remains were mostly deposited in the sea, not on land. Since dinosaurs did not live in the ocean, it took special circumstances for their remains to be deposited there. Fortunately for paleontologists, an occasional carcass was carried downstream into the ocean, perhaps as the result of an accidental drowning in a storm-swollen stream. Similar events are observed today in the African wilderness when herds of migrating wildebeest, for example, cross a flooding river only to have numerous individuals drown in the process and their carcasses carried downstream. In San Diego the marine Cretaceous rocks containing dinosaur remains were uplifted and exposed as a result of active faulting and erosion. Note that

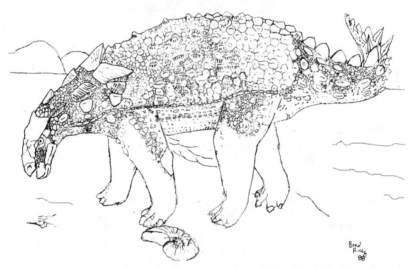

Figure 3.14. Hypothetical reconstruction of the Carlsbad nodosaur showing arrangement of bony "skin" armor plates. Reconstruction and drawing by Brad Riney.

the large marine reptiles of Mesozoic time were not dinosaurs, but were differing types of reptiles such as plesiosaurs, ichthyosaurs, and mosasaurs; dinosaurs dominated the land and took to the air but did not live in the ocean.

Cretaceous Field Trip:
Shallow- to Deep-Marine Strata Around La Jolla Bay to La Jolla Cove

A beautiful coastal walk around La Jolla Bay to La Jolla Cove provides intriguing glimpses into late Cretaceous conditions in San Diego (but first check the tide charts—the early part of this walk is best done during a minus tide). We are going to walk along the rocky beach south of the La Jolla Beach and Tennis Club (Figure 3.3). We will walk through the Rose Canyon fault zone, experience sea caves, use a rope to help climb up the steep slope on the Country Club fault of the Rose Canyon fault zone, and view interesting Cretaceous fossils and sedimentary rocks. After all this excitement, we will mingle with the masses of people at La Jolla Cove.

Begin by parking along Paseo Dorado (Figure 3.15; and *Thomas Guide,* p. 1227, G5); walk to the beach using the public-access walkway on the southern side of the Marine Room at the La Jolla Beach and Tennis Club. Walk southwest along the seawall that hides the Cretaceous sandstone beds and the active faults of the Rose Canyon fault zone. At the end of the seawall, wade across the surge channel (an almost dry walk during a minus tide), and go around the bend to find a charming sandy cove. Exposed here are coarse sandstones of the Point Loma Formation. The sandstones are composed of subequal amounts of quartz and feldspar plus small fragments of plutonic rocks, biotite mica, and other minerals. The sandstones contain a variety of features that tell of shallow marine water with reversing current flow (Figure 3.16). In other words, at this spot 76 million years ago, the environment was similar to what you are walking and wading through today. As you look at the sandstone, notice the following:

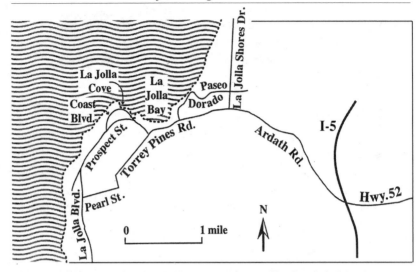

Figure 3.15. Map for La Jolla Bay to La Jolla Cove field trip.

- Small-scale cross bedding (herringbone structure) where ancient ripples (sand waves) moved back and forth leaving a pattern crudely reminiscent of a herringbone fabric.
- Alternating light- and dark-colored laminae (thin layers of sediment) formed where water currents rolled light-colored quartz and feldspar sand grains until the current lost energy or reversed direction.
- Dark biotite mica flakes, which dropped from suspension in the water under low-energy conditions.
- Burrows made by invertebrate organisms as homes or in their search for food in soft sediment (now turned to rock).
- Pieces of shells from fossil clams, snails, and rudistid clams (a hadrosaur vertebra was found here).
- Small faults offsetting the rock layers.

Proceed southwest along the cliffs. If you walk into some of the narrow fractures in the cliff, you can enter sea caves and continue your walk underground. On the last massive cliff face of sandstone, notice the thick sandstone beds that cease quite abruptly and are

*Figure 3.16. Shallow-marine sandstone of the Point Loma Forma-
tion at La Jolla Bay. Numerous scour surfaces and cross beds
(inclined thin layers of sediment) formed as small dunes moved
about the shallow sea floor.*

overlain by fine-grained mudstone and the well-developed faults of
the Rose Canyon fault system in the last cliff face.

Walk onto the gravel beach and inspect the lowest dark bed
sitting on top of the sandstone. The bed is loaded with fossil fragments of many kinds of organisms—clams, snails, oysters, corals,
bryozoans, brachiopods, echinoids (sea urchin spines), and many
more types of marine invertebrates (Figure 3.17). This is a "condensed bed" where slow depositional rates of sediment have allowed
numerous skeletons to accumulate, be crunched to pieces by scav-
enging organisms, and become chemically stained before burial. The
bed also marks a stunning change in water depth. Face the cliff and
put your left hand on the uppermost sandstone layer, then place
your right hand on the mudstone above the shell-rich condensed
bed. Your left hand is touching sandstone deposited in water 1-meter
deep, and your right hand is touching mudstone deposited in water

Figure 3.17. Abundantly fossiliferous sandstone at base of deep-water mudstone at La Jolla Bay. This sandstone is a "condensed bed" where sand deposition rates were so slow that the remains of many generations of organisms were left behind as fossils.

1,000-meters deep. The stunning change in water depth must have been caused by ancient fault movements that offset the ocean floor and created the rapid deepening of seawater.

As you walk south along the rocky shore, notice the following:

- Dipping sedimentary rock layers on the modern wave-cut platform (Figure 3.18); remember that these sedimentary rocks were deposited as horizontal layers before being deformed by movements of the Rose Canyon fault system.
- Fine-grained mudstones in the sea cliff, with the gray color imparted by the finely comminuted organic debris they contain (Figure 3.19).

Figure 3.18. View southwest, toward La Jolla Cove, over dipping deep-marine sedimentary beds on the wave-cut platform around La Jolla Bay. Originally horizontal sedimentary layers have been tilted by movements along the Rose Canyon fault zone.

Figure 3.19. View east along south shore of La Jolla Bay showing cliffs cut into mudstone layers that dip toward the south.

- Microscopic fossils (foraminifera, coccoliths), which are abundant in these bathyal-depth mudstones (accumulated at a water depth of 0.6 mile [1 km]); you may also find coiled and straight ammonites (Figure 3.9) and large inoceramid clam shells (Figure 3.10).

How stable are the rock foundations beneath the million-dollar houses on top of the cliffs?

As your path swings toward the west, notice that some sandstone beds appear in the cliffs (Figure 3.20). Check the sandstones for features indicating that they were deposited when gravity-pulled submarine turbidity currents began losing their energy; for example, notice the following:

- Graded bedding resulting from the coarsest sediment grains dropping first, followed by progressively finer grains.

Figure 3.20. View east along south shore of La Jolla Bay showing sandstone and mudstone beds of the outer part of the submarine fan. A close look at the sandstone beds reveals grading of grain sizes.

- Broken shells of extinct reef-building rudistid clams.
- Thin layers of small, black, carbonized wood chips that became saturated in nearshore shallow seawater before being carried to deep water by turbidity currents. Scott Curran has analyzed these fossilized wood fragments and shown that the blackening is due, not to fires, but to the initial stages of coal formation.

Continuing west you will run out of beach; stop to face a steep cliff made of sandstone layers. Why are these massive sandstone layers so different and discontinuous from the mudstone layers found on the east side? You are looking at rock layers offset by the Country Club fault of the Rose Canyon fault zone. You can look closely at the fault surface and see grooves (slickensides) that formed along planar surfaces in the rocks when they were "scratched" during fault movement as the west-side block of the fault (downtown La Jolla) moved northward.

Using the rope, climb up the Country Club fault to the scenic Coast Walk trail. Be careful! Stand on the footbridge and look at the new million-dollar homes built on top of the Country Club fault Enjoy the stroll west on Coast Walk as you pass the cliff known as Deadman's Leap (don't get any foolish ideas here) on your way to Coast Boulevard and La Jolla Cove. After walking partway downhill on Coast Boulevard, stop and look back east to the La Jolla Bay traverse you have just completed (Figure 3.21).

At La Jolla Cove, the sea cliffs expose sandstone beds that filled channels on the middle part of the Cretaceous submarine fan (Figures 3.6 and 3.22). Each sandstone bed originated as a fluidized flow—a submarine, gravity-pulled flow, sort of like downslope-moving quicksand. A close inspection of a sandstone bed may reveal the following:

- Flame structures (Figure 2.4).
- De-watering structures, such as "dishes" and fluid-escape pipes, that were created when the water within the moving sand mass oozed upward and out, causing the friction between the sand grains to increase and ultimately stop the sand mass.
- Load structures where heavy sand beds partially sank and/or injected into underlying weak muds (Figure 2.4).

Figure 3.21. View eastward across La Jolla Bay. In foreground are thick sandstone beds of the Point Loma Formation that accumulated in broad channels in the middle of a submarine fan.

Figure 3.22. Sandstone beds of the Point Loma Formation that were deposited in a middle fan channel on the late Cretaceous submarine fan, west of La Jolla Cove.

62

These channel-filling sandstones from the middle portion of the-submarine fan persist southward down the coast to just south of Bird Rock. Gravels accumulated in the inner-fan valley high on the submarine fan; they may be seen as conglomerates in the beach cliffs south of Bird Rock and around False Point (Figure 3.23). When you look at the conglomerate clasts, remember that these volcanic- and plutonic-igneous rocks, as well as the metamorphic rock clasts, are pieces of the erosion-reduced ancestral Peninsular Ranges formed earlier in Cretaceous time.

Cretaceous Field Trip: Submarine Fan Strata on Southern Point Loma

Southern Point Loma presents other interesting features in the Cretaceous marine strata. Drive down Cabrillo Road, park in the lot above the Point Loma tidepools, and walk down to the tidepools

Figure 3.23. Cabrillo Formation conglomerate deposited in the inner-fan valley of the late Cretaceous submarine fan, at False Point.

(Figure 3.24; and *Thomas Guide,* p. 1308, A3). In the tidepools area, each low tide exposes many thin beds of mudstone and sandstone of the Point Loma Formation; these beds accumulated in the middle part of the submarine fan, outside and alongside the sandstone-filled channels seen at La Jolla Cove. The muds were deposited in half-mile-deep water as clays, fine silts, and organic detritus settled from suspension in seawater. The organic material in the mud

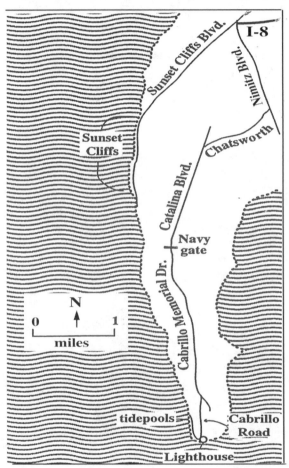

Figure 3.24. Map for southern Point Loma field trip.

was a rich source of food for sediment-swallowing organisms like worms, arthropods, and others that burrowed through the sediment leaving their trails and traces behind them (Figures 3.25 and 3.26). Walk around on the upper surfaces of the mudstone beds and look closely. How many types of burrows can you find? Can you figure

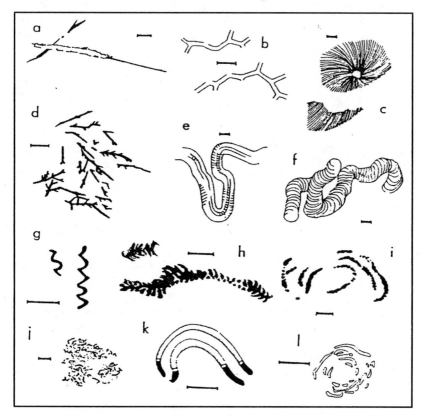

Figure 3.25. Fossil traces of burrows and grazing tracks, Point Loma tidepools area. (a) Ophiomorpha, (b) Thalassinoides, (c) Zoophycos, (d) Chondrites, (e, f) Scolicia, (g) Belorhaphe, (h) Nereites, (i) Spirophycos, (j, k, l) *unidentified burrows. Black bar with each sample is 0.8 inch (2 cm) long, except bar for fossil b, which is 6 inches (15 cm) long. From Kern and Warme, 1974.*

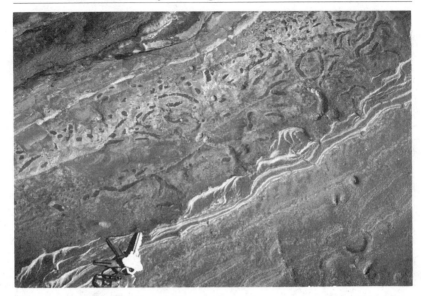

Figure 3.26. Trace fossils, Spirophycos *and* Zoophycos, *at Point Loma tidepools. Keys for scale.*

out what kind of organism made each trace fossil? What types of movements did each make? Were they trying to obtain nourishment or shelter? Both types of activity are preserved here.

Take a look at Figure 3.7 and notice that *above* the conglomerate in the Cabrillo Formation is another thick package of sandstone; this sandstone is not present in the beach cliffs at Bird Rock but is readily seen on the southern tip of Point Loma. Remember, the sands were deposited in deeper water farther from the shoreline than were the gravels. On Point Loma, the upward change from conglomerate back to sandstone suggests that an ocean-deepening event occurred. A clue to what happened is available at the base of the Cabrillo Formation sandstone, which is exposed in the left-hand roadcut at the toll-booth entry to Cabrillo National Monument (Figure 3.27). Present in a discontinuous layer are extra-large boulders of Santiago Peak Volcanics. This concentration of boulders along one bed suggests that faulting offset the submarine fan, causing the ocean to deepen and a steep subsea fault scarp (cliff) to form, exposing basement rock (Santiago Peak Volcanics); large hunks of Santiago Peak Volcanics fell from the fault scarp directly onto the submarine fan.

Figure 3.27. Large clast of Santiago Peak Volcanics at base of upper sandstone in Cabrillo Formation at entrance to Cabrillo National Monument. Brad Steer for scale.

CHAPTER 4
PALEOCENE HISTORY

In 1874 the German botanist Wilhelm Philipp Schimper recognized a distinct fossil plant assemblage that was younger than Cretaceous but older than Eocene. He referred to this interval as the Paleocene and defined a type section for these sedimentary rocks that lies just northeast of Paris, France. The significant changes that occurred 65 million years ago in plant and animal groups, including the extinction of most dinosaurs, are now recognized as one of the largest mass extinctions in Earth history. This event marked the close of Cretaceous time. Paleocene time occurred 65 to 55 million years ago and marks a reorganization and repopulation of life on Earth.

Tectonics
In the San Diego region, Paleocene time is notable for its absence of igneous rocks. For tens of millions of years during Jurassic and most of Cretaceous time, the San Diego region received huge volumes of magma from the Earth's interior. The solidified Jurassic and Cretaceous magmas comprise the plutonic-rock dominated Peninsular Ranges and their volcanic-rock foothills to the west. But the magma production stopped in the San Diego region as the oceanic plate shallowed its angle of subduction and passed beneath the western edge of the North American continent without penetrating into the

asthenosphere at 60-miles depth. Asthenosphere penetration occurred progressively farther to the east, and the sites of volcanism moved eastward with it into what is now Arizona and New Mexico. Consequently, neither plutonic nor volcanic rocks of Paleocene age are found in San Diego.

Paleocene Sedimentary Record

The interval of time between about 70 and 55 million years ago (the latest Cretaceous and the Paleocene) is not well represented in the rocks of the San Diego region. During this time, erosion both destroyed formerly existing rocks and kept sediments and organic remains from being deposited. One spectacular event of this time missing from the San Diego rock record is the effect of a large asteroid that hit the Yucatan Peninsula of Mexico 65 million years ago. The lack of rocks of this age prevents us from seeing how the asteroid affected San Diego; for example, what kind and amount of airborne debris blanketed our area? what damages resulted from the tsunami (giant sea waves) generated by the impact of the asteroid? and what species may have been driven to extinction?

Paleosols (Ancient Soils)

What do we know about the very latest Cretaceous, Paleocene, and earliest Eocene history of San Diego? Not much. Although few sediments were deposited and preserved during this time, the exposed land surface was subject to weathering that produced soils. The San Diego region has an impressive accumulation of ancient soils (called *paleosols*) buried beneath middle Eocene sedimentary rocks (50–37 million years old) and preserved in the rock record. Just as the composition of modern soils is controlled by the climatic conditions under which they form, so were ancient soils formed based on the climatic regimes of their time. If more than one climatic regime occurred during a geologically long time of exposure, the most severe of those climates is the one best preserved in the rock record. A severe climate causes more intense and voluminous decomposition of surface rock that more recent and milder climatic conditions cannot erase.

How do soils form? The rocks exposed at Earth's surface physically disintegrate and chemically decompose over time, yielding a zone of weathered rock known as soil. The processes involved in disintegration and decomposition are called *mechanical weathering* and *chemical weathering.*

Processes of physical disintegration (mechanical weathering) include the following:

- Thermal expansion and contraction. The daily expansion of rocks due to solar heating, and contraction on cooling, causes microcracks to form in the rock; these cracks increase in number and size over time, causing the rock to crumble.
- Freezing water. Water fills cracks in rocks; when it freezes, it expands in volume by 9%. The pressure of expanding ice crystals acts like innumerable levers or jacks prying rocks apart.
- Root wedging. As plants grow, their roots become longer and thicker. The wedging action of roots breaks rocks apart in the same way it breaks apart sidewalks, concrete curbs, and roads.

The collective action of mechanical weathering processes takes the massive rocks exposed at the Earth's surface and breaks them into smaller pieces. The smaller a rock becomes, the greater its surface-area-to-volume ratio, and thus the greater its susceptibility to chemical weathering. Chemicals attack surfaces, and because smaller rocks have greater surface areas, they are more prone to chemical weathering. The decomposition of rocks near the Earth's surface is mostly carried out by surface waters (rain, lakes, and streams) that have been pulled underground by gravity. This groundwater attacks the rock surfaces it touches, dissolving some minerals, selectively leaching others, and leaving some minerals effectively unchanged.

Water is commonly referred to as the "universal solvent," but it does not accomplish chemical decomposition alone. Virtually all water (H_2O) contains carbon dioxide (CO_2) absorbed from the atmosphere or from plant sources; when combined, these molecules form carbonic acid (H_2CO_3), which intensifies the process of decomposition. (We consume carbonic acid every time we drink a carbonated beverage, which is made by dissolving CO_2 in H_2O and adding sugar and flavoring.)

The effects of mechanical and chemical weathering combine to produce a set of loose materials at Earth's surface that differ from fresh, unweathered parent rock. By finding out which elements and minerals have been removed or added, we can learn about the ancient climatic conditions prevailing at a particular time.

During their development, soils form distinct horizons, or zones, that vary with depth. The uppermost zone, including the ground surface, is the *A* horizon, or zone of leaching. In this zone, soluble minerals and clays are moved downward while organic material gathers. The next layer down is the *B* horizon, or zone of accumulation. In this zone iron oxides and carbonate minerals precipitate and washed-down clay minerals accumulate. The next layer down is the *C* horizon, or zone of partially disintegrated and decomposed parent rock or bedrock.

PALEOCENE PALEOSOL LOCALITIES

In San Diego, remnants of a once-widespread ancient soil (*paleosol*) that formed during Paleocene and early Eocene time are preserved beneath middle Eocene (about 50 million years ago) sedimentary rocks. This paleosol lies on the now-buried land surface of a rugged ancient landscape. From the law of superposition we know that this paleosol must be older than the middle Eocene rocks that were deposited on top of it. The paleosol developed on top of a variety of different rock types and can be found at numerous locations, including the following:

- On top of early Cretaceous-age Santiago Peak Volcanics at (1) Camp Pendleton Marine Corps Base, (2) around the Rancho Peñasquitos housing area, and (3) on Del Cerro and the San Diego State University campus (Abbott, 1981).
- On top of mid-Cretaceous-age plutonic rocks along Finch Street in El Cajon and on Rancho Delicias south of Tijuana.
- On top of the late Cretaceous-age Point Loma Formation just north of McClellan Palomar Airport in Carlsbad (Figure 4.1).
- On top of the Mount Soledad Formation deposited in latest Paleocene and earliest Eocene time and now found at the mouth of Indian Trail Canyon at Black's Beach (Peterson and Abbott, 1979).

Figure 4.1. Cretaceous Point Loma Formation conglomerate just north of McClellan Palomar Airport. The shape and texture of the gravels are easily seen, yet the gravels remain only as "ghosts" or relicts; mineralogically they have been completely decomposed, in place, to a kaolinite-clay paleosol.

The Paleocene paleosols are being destroyed by urbanization, though some can still be found in the area. Three of the best remaining exposures can be seen in the following locations:

- On the northeast side of the San Diego State University campus (*Thomas Guide,* p. 1270, C1); the lower part of the roadcut on Canyon Crest Drive (next to Interstate 8) just north of the SDSU art building exposes volcanic rocks (andesitic breccias) of the early Cretaceous Santiago Peak Volcanics. High on the roadcut are Eocene sandstones dipping off to the west; buried beneath the Eocene strata is a paleosol—a brick-red remnant (3 feet [1 m] thick by 23 feet [7 m] long) of *B*-horizon paleosol colored by abundant iron oxides (ancient "rust"). Below the red paleosol is a thick interval (55 feet [17 m]) of severely weathered Santiago Peak Volcanics representing the *C* horizon of the paleosol.

- At Rancho Delicias, south of Tijuana in Baja California, the paleosol developed from granodiorite, a type of plutonic igneous rock (Figure 4.2). Most of the granodiorite minerals were either dissolved or transformed to kaolinite clay through chemical weathering (Table 4.1); the only original mineral remaining is quartz, and the exterior surfaces of its grains have been chemically corroded.
- At the mouth of Indian Trail Canyon at Black's Beach (be aware that Black's Beach is dominated by nude beach-goers), an outcrop of Eocene Mount Soledad Formation is severely weathered into a paleosol (*Thomas Guide*, p. 1207, stream mouth in upper quarter of H7). The top of the Eocene conglomerate is a 3-foot (1 m) thick remnant of white *A*-horizon paleosol that escaped erosion when the overlying middle Eocene sandstone was being deposited (Figure 4.3). The *A*-horizon paleosol is dominated by the clay mineral kaolinite. Below the white clay is an interval

Figure 4.2. Thick tropical soil (white) buried beneath middle Eocene marine sandstone and mudstone at Rancho Delicias, south of Tijuana, Baja California.

Granodiorite parent rock		Ancient soil	
Plagioclase feldspar	43%	Kaolinite	66%
Quartz	20%	Quartz	33%
Orthoclase feldspar	20%	Iron oxides	1%
Hornblende	9%		
Biotite mica	6%		
Accessory minerals	2%		

Table 4.1. Mineralogy of rocks at Rancho Delicias, Baja California. From Abbott, Minch, and Peterson, 1976.

several yards thick of thoroughly rotted Mount Soledad Formation conglomerate (*C* horizon). All of the conglomerate clasts, except those few composed mostly of quartz (such as quartzite, pegmatite, and silicified volcanic ash), are decomposed in place. (This outcrop is discussed in Chapter 5 in the Eocene Marine Field Trip, Indian Trail Canyon stop.)

PALEOSOL CHARACTERISTICS

Although the paleosol developed on top of different types of parent rocks—namely, (1) andesitic volcanic rock (Santiago Peak Volcanics), (2) granitic rock (Peninsular Ranges plutonic rocks), (3) conglomerate with clasts of mixed rock types (Point Loma Formation), and (4) sandstone and rhyolitic volcanic clast-dominated conglomerate (Mount Soledad Formation)—its composition is nearly identical in all locations. This finding implies that long lengths of time with severe chemical weathering were required to remove the same elements from all the rocks, regardless of their composition, resulting in an essentially homogeneous soil.

What is the composition of the paleosol? Typically the upper part of the soil zone is composed of a simple mineral assemblage:

about one-third quartz grains (silicon dioxide), two-thirds kaolinite clay (aluminum silicate), and a small amount of iron oxide. The unique aspect of this limited mineral assemblage is its restricted chemical composition—quartz, which is silicon dioxide (SiO_2); kaolinite, which is an aluminum silicate ($Al_4Si_4O_{10}(OH)_8$); and iron oxide (Fe_2O_3). Removed during weathering are the common and abundant elements sodium, calcium, potassium, magnesium, and numerous less common and trace elements; in other words, this soil has been severely leached.

Figure 4.3. Ancient tropical soil at the mouth of Indian Trail Canyon at Black's Beach. The rock below the arrows is badly weathered late Paleocene to early Eocene Mount Soledad Formation conglomerate. The whitish band immediately below the arrows is A-horizon paleosol composed of kaolinite with residual quartz grains. The cliff face beneath the A horizon is the upper part of the C horizon. The rock above the paleosol is a sandstone body that accumulated in a submarine canyon in middle Eocene time; the sandstone was deposited on top of the erosion surface that removed much of the paleosol.

The kaolinite clay found in the region is exceptionally pure and has been mined near McClellan Palomar Airport and continues to be mined at Rancho Delicias. Kaolinite is used, for example, as the main constituent in many ceramics, as coatings on paper, and as a filler in medicines.

PALEOCENE CLIMATE

What does this ancient soil reveal? It tells us that the climate in San Diego during Paleocene time was humid, tropical, and long-enduring. Geologists make inferences about ancient climates by extrapolating from modern-day climatic conditions (rainfall and temperature) in locations where modern-day soils of the same composition and thickness as the paleosols are found.

The interpretation of climatic conditions under which San Diego's paleosols were formed is based on the extreme degree of chemical leaching and the great thickness of the soil profile. At Rancho Delicias, for example, the paleosol is overlain by mid-Eocene marine shelf mudstone (Figure 4.2). An unknown thickness of the paleosol was eroded away by the Eocene sea, yet the remaining kaolinite is more than 40 feet (12 m) thick in the *A* horizon, and below it lies another 50 feet (15 m) of C-horizon decomposed bedrock. Today, soils this thick and this severely depleted of chemical constituents form only in the tropics. We can estimate the ancient climate by finding where soils of the same composition and thickness exist today, seeing what rainfall and temperature conditions exist there, and then extrapolating these numbers back to the ancient conditions in San Diego. Gary Peterson and I have estimated that the average annual temperature in San Diego during Paleocene to early Eocene time was at least 73°F (compared with 61°F today) (Figure 4.4), and the average annual rainfall was greater than 60 inches per year (compared with less than 10 inches per year today).

Why did San Diego have a tropical climate at this time? The first hypothesis to evaluate involves plate tectonics and drifting continents. Was San Diego at a tropical latitude 60 to 55 million years ago? The answer is no—San Diego was actually farther north at that time, at about the latitude of present-day San Francisco.

AVERAGE ANNUAL RAINFALL (INCHES)

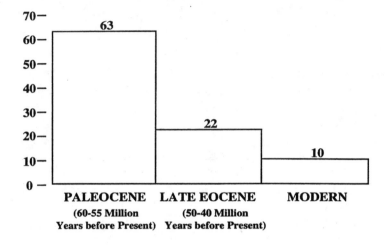

AVERAGE ANNUAL TEMPERATURE (°F)

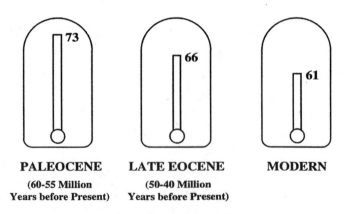

Figure 4.4. Average annual rainfall and temperature in San Diego for three different time periods.

Another hypothesis to evaluate involves the global climatic conditions in Paleocene time. Here we have success, for it turns out that the Paleocene Earth simply had a warmer climate. During this climatic interval, called a "Torrid Age," the global climate was warmer and the tropical climatic belt was much wider than today. The polar climate, for example, was equable enough for palm trees to grow and alligators to dwell inside the Arctic Circle.

The extra-warm Earth seen during the Paleocene Torrid Age is hard for us to imagine because climatic conditions today are unusual in Earth's climatic history. We are living during an Ice Age. Just 15,000 years ago, 27% of Earth's continental area was buried beneath massive ice sheets; and even though we are now in an interglacial episode, 10% of the continental area (namely Antarctica and Greenland) is still beneath ice. What seems ordinary to us, because it is the world we live in, is actually extraordinary. Just as Earth's climatic pendulum has now swung to the cold side, there are times when it swings to the hot side. Since early Eocene time, there has been a general decline in global temperature and an increase in climatic differences between the latitudes.

CHAPTER 5
EOCENE HISTORY

The Eocene is an interval of Earth history first recognized by the Englishman Charles Lyell in 1829 and described in his influential textbook *Principles of Geology*. Lyell subdivided the Cenozoic strata "in chronological order, by reference to the comparative proportion of living species of shells found in each." The best exposures of Eocene strata that Lyell studied are his type areas in the Paris and London basins where about 3.5% of species represented in fossils are still alive today.

Eocene time is now defined as having occurred 55 to 33.7 million years ago. The San Diego region has world-renowned exposures of Eocene nonmarine and marine sedimentary rocks and fossils.

Tectonics

By Eocene time, subduction of the oceanic plate (Farallon plate) had been occurring along western North America for tens of millions of years. The subduction process built the impressive Cretaceous-age mountains of the ancestral Peninsular Ranges. As shown in Figure 3.1, the oceanic plate reaching San Diego in mid-Cretaceous time subducted at a steep angle, causing copious volumes of magma to move upward from a depth of 60 miles. The subducting oceanic plate was old, cold, and dense, and gravity pulled it into the Earth at a steep angle.

What happened to the Cretaceous mountain-building process? As time moved on, North America drifted farther westward and overran progressively younger portions of the oceanic plate (Pacific Ocean floor) that were warmer, less dense, and more buoyant. The increasing buoyancy of the oceanic plate made subduction more difficult, resulting in a progressive shallowing of the angle of subduction of the downward-moving plate from late Cretaceous through Eocene time (Figure 5.1). As the downgoing oceanic plate moved eastward at progressively shallower depths, it no longer penetrated deep enough beneath California to release magma, and thus the pluton-forming, mountain-building process was shut off in the Californias. The process of mountain building moved eastward into states such as Arizona and New Mexico as the oceanic plate was underthrust farther beneath western North America in an event known as the Laramide Orogeny. Meanwhile, the forces of erosion continued to severely reduce the size of the Cretaceous mountains of the ancestral Peninsular Ranges of the Californias.

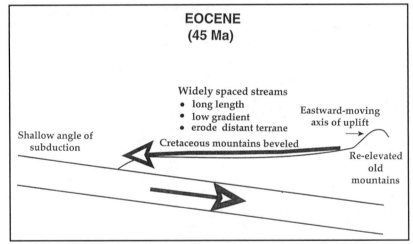

Figure 5.1. In Eocene time (45 million years ago), the young and buoyant oceanic plate subducted eastward at a shallow angle beneath the California region. No magma was forming under San Diego then, rivers lengthened their courses greatly, and the Cretaceous mountains were eroded down to a relatively flat surface.

Eocene Climate and Paleogeography

Eocene time was an interval of major climatic and biologic change. The Eocene began as a continuation of the Paleocene torrid age with warm climates extending from the equator to very high latitudes. Polar icecaps were nonexistent, global sea level was high, and the edges of continents were flooded. Entering Eocene time, the oceans and continents were configured differently than they are today (Figure 5.2). Notable features of Eocene Earth include (1) the absence of circumpolar, southern, and Arctic oceans; (2) remnants of the circumequatorial ocean known as the Tethys Sea; (3) India had yet to collide with Asia; and (4) Central America not yet fully formed. Eocene oceanic currents moved along routes different from today,

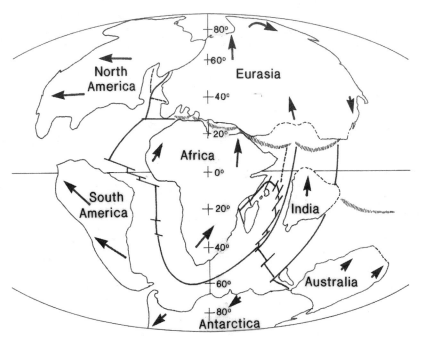

Figure 5.2. Continents and oceans before Eocene time. The modern world is becoming recognizable. North America has yet to finalize its divorce from Europe, and Australia is still part of Antarctica.

and the ocean was sluggish due to warm water temperatures that were similar at all depths and latitudes worldwide, unlike today. Primary biologic productivity was greatest in the equatorial zone.

Torrid climatic intervals occurred during Paleocene and Eocene time, but by the close of the Eocene, the world climate had begun the long cooling trend that led to the Ice Age we live in today.

Mammalian Evolution

Although mammals coexisted with the ruling reptiles throughout most of Mesozoic time (Figure 1.5), they remained a relatively minor group of small-bodied animals with limited diversity and a generally nocturnal lifestyle. All this changed dramatically following the mass extinction that closed out Cretaceous time. Gone were the big-bodied dinosaurs that dominated the land; gone also were the large marine reptiles. Paleocene time dawned with a wide variety of open habitats, both on land and in the seas. Mammalian survivors included multituberculates, archaic marsupials, and primitive insectivores. Changes in these mammals over time resulted in new types of mammals that began successfully filling the empty niches in the environment. This evolutionary explosion included a number of major types of mammals that went extinct within several millions of years, but it also included the earliest representatives of living groups such as bats, primates, rodents, tapirs, rhinos, horses, whales, sea cows, and elephants.

MULTITUBERCULATES

Although the mammals living with the dinosaurs during Mesozoic time had small bodies, they had already developed enlarged brains, specialized teeth, and good hearing. The multituberculates (called "multis") were a successful group of early mammals (Order Multituberculata); many species evolved that spread far and wide. The fossils of these shrew-sized animals have been found in rocks as old as 212 million years. Multituberculates had distinctive sets of teeth with large incisors, giving them a look vaguely reminiscent of rodents; however, multis had been around for over 150 million years before rodents first appeared. In San Diego, multituberculate teeth have been collected by Steve Walsh in Tertiary-age rocks along

Morena Boulevard. Some species of multis moved quickly about the ground, and others lived in trees. These widespread, well-adapted little mammals survived the mass extinction 65 million years ago, but their luck ended about 35 million years ago as extinction befell them near the close of Eocene time. After existing for 180 million years and surviving the mass extinction that claimed the dinosaurs, why did multis go extinct? Maybe they were unable to handle the competition from the new kids in the neighborhood—the rodents.

Changing Sea Levels

One of the major controls on sediment deposition is the position of the shoreline. A worldwide rise in sea level will cause depositional environments to migrate inland, and a worldwide drop in sea level will cause them to move seaward. During Eocene time, global sea level both rose and fell (Figure 5.3).

Two major variables governed the deposition of Eocene sedimentary rock bodies in San Diego: (1) sea level rise and fall, and (2) the westward growth of the massive Poway alluvial fan. Through most of middle Eocene time, sea level rose until the shoreline was up against the mountains at what is now Lakeside and Olivenhain. The shallow marine environments moved landward, and the coarse sands and gravels were deposited near the shoreline, well inland to the east. But even against a rising sea level, the westward growth of the Poway alluvial fan caused by massive volumes of sediments being deposited was so powerful that it built out seaward, pushing the shoreline to the west. In Figure 5.3, notice that earlier in Eocene time the sedimentary formations migrated landward with rising sea level; also notice the massive alluvial fan of the Poway Conglomerate that built out seaward and overwhelmed the high sea level. The sedimentary result was the creation of a "chevron" pattern of Eocene formations, as shown in the schematic cross section in Figure 5.3.

Eocene Formations

The Eocene sedimentary rocks in San Diego were divided into two major groups—the La Jolla Group and the Poway Group—by Mike Kennedy and George Moore in 1971 (Figure 5.4).

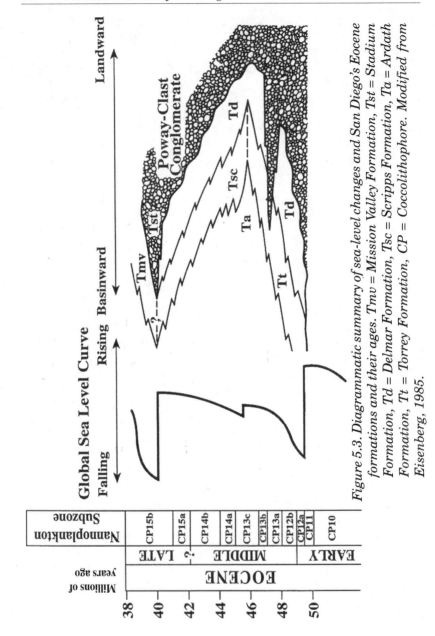

Figure 5.3. Diagrammatic summary of sea-level changes and San Diego's Eocene formations and their ages. Tmv = Mission Valley Formation, Tst = Stadium Formation, Td = Delmar Formation, Tsc = Scripps Formation, Ta = Ardath Formation, Tt = Torrey Formation, CP = Coccolithophore. Modified from Eisenberg, 1985.

The La Jolla Group is composed mostly of sediments accumulated in coastal-plain environments shown in Figure 5.5 as lagoon (Delmar Formation), tidal flats and beach (Torrey Sandstone), and continental shelf (Ardath Shale). Ancient tidal channels are mostly filled by sandstone that displays multiple erosion surfaces, reflecting the changing tides, and by cross bedding formed as inclined thin layers of sand were deposited on the front sides of sand bars (Figure 5.6). Times of subaerial exposure are shown by flat mudstone surfaces with polygonal sun-shrinkage cracks filled by slightly younger sands (Figure 5.7). In the lagoon, oysters covered marsh flats (Figure 5.8), roots of salt water–tolerant trees found anchorage (Figure 5.9), and tree leaves were buried (Figures 5.10 and 5.11).

The Poway Group is composed mostly of sediment brought by the ancient Ballena river to build the Eocene Poway alluvial fan and associated sedimentary deposits (Figure 5.12). These rhyolitic gravel- and sand-bearing formations include the Stadium, Mission Valley, and Pomerado Formations. Remembering that formations take their names from geographic features near good exposures of the rock mass, can you estimate where these formations got their names? (For the answers, see Kennedy and Moore, 1971).

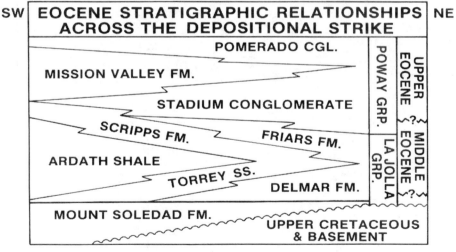

Figure 5.4. Cross section showing vertical relationships of Eocene formations in San Diego. After Kennedy and Moore, 1971.

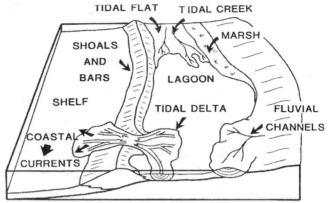

Figure 5.5. Block diagram showing Eocene depositional environments in northern San Diego area. From Lohmar, May, Boyer, and Warme, 1979.

Figure 5.6. Stacked tidal-channel sandstone beds, Solana Beach cliffs.

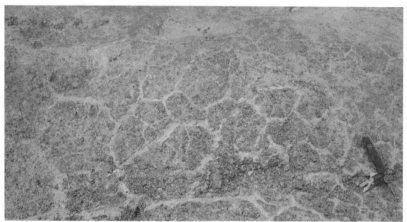

Figure 5.7. Sand-filled sun-shrinkage cracks in Eocene mudstone, south Carlsbad beach cliffs.

Figure 5.8. Oyster beds in Delmar Formation, Solana Beach cliffs.

89

Figure 5.9. Rooted stump in Delmar Formation, Torrey Pines State Beach.

Figure 5.10. Fragment of Eocene palm frond collected near Del Mar.

Figure 5.11. Eocene Ficus leaf collected near Del Mar.

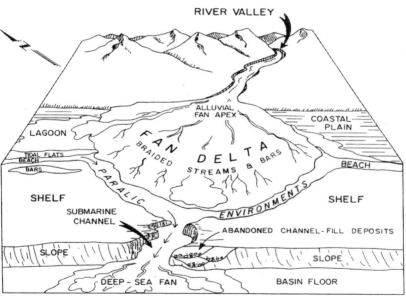

Figure 5.12. Eocene depositional environments in San Diego. From Link, Peterson, and Abbott, 1979.

Eocene Nonmarine Field Trip:
Ramona–San Vicente Reservoir Area

One of the most striking features of the Peninsular Ranges is their relatively flat top. Visualize driving east on Interstate 8 from San Diego to the top of the mountains around Boulevard—look north, then look south into Baja California—what do you see? A rather flat surface, a moderately rolling terrain with a few scattered hills or small peaks rising above it. Where are the high, sharp mountain peaks separated by steep, V-shaped valleys one would expect, as in the Sierra Nevada? The top of the Peninsular Ranges does not look like a mountain range; instead it looks like an old erosion surface that has been elevated well above sea level.

When was this erosion surface produced? The mid-Cretaceous mountain mass was lowered significantly by erosion (remember the Cretaceous Lusardi and Cabrillo conglomerates) under a climate that was tropical at times (remember the Paleocene paleosols). By middle Eocene time a large river flowed over the area that we now observe as linear outcrops of Eocene conglomerate (the Ballena Gravels) associated with the erosion surface (Figure 5.13). Coarse sediments deposited in the Eocene Ballena river and on the apex of the Poway alluvial fan can be seen in Ramona and the San Vicente Reservoir area (Figure 5.14).

Eocene Ballena River

Lying in an ancient valley cut into the erosion surface between Santa Ysabel and San Vicente Reservoir to the southwest is an elongate, east-northeast to west-southwest oriented ancient river channel containing middle Eocene conglomerate (Figure 5.13). This conglomerate was first described in 1892 by H. W. Fairbanks, who recognized that the conglomerate was deposited in an ancient river valley. He named the deposit the Ballena Gravels (*ballena* is Spanish for whale) and studied them for their economic potential, trying to learn if they were gold-bearing like the Eocene river deposits in the Sierra Nevada. Because the Eocene river gravels in San Diego are preserved as far east as Whale Peak (to the west of Santa Ysabel

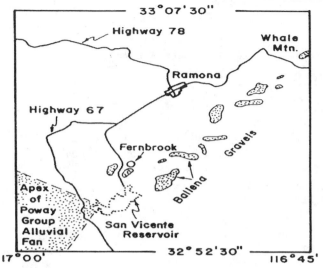

Figure 5.13. Outcrop map of the Eocene Ballena Gravels and apex of the Poway fan. From Steer and Abbott, 1984.

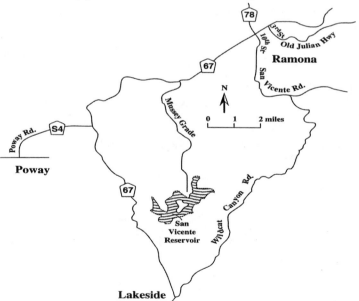

Figure 5.14. Map of the Ramona–Poway–Lakeside area.

Valley), Fairbanks felt that the river came from east of the Peninsular Ranges. For a large river to flow across the Peninsular Ranges from the east, the landscape had to have been very different from the landscape of today; for example, the old erosion surface must have been at a lower elevation, and the Gulf of California–Salton Trough depression did not yet exist.

Where were the headwaters of the Eocene Ballena river? To answer this question one must first have an understanding of where landmasses were positioned during Eocene time. The Gulf of California, for example, is a geologically young feature—it is only 5.5 million years old. Before the Gulf of California opened, San Diego was adjacent to the present-day state of Sonora in northwestern Mexico. During the last 5.5 million years the block of Baja California–San Diego–Los Angeles has been moving northward, crossing 2.5 degrees of latitude, opening the Gulf of California in the process. One way to see for yourself the effects of this opening is to use scissors on a map; cut along the San Andreas fault and then slide the western piece to the south, removing the Gulf of California and realigning Baja California with mainland Mexico; this places San Diego adjacent to the present day state of Sonora in northwestern Mexico.

SOURCE OF THE BALLENA RIVER

How can we determine if the Eocene Ballena river flowed from Sonora, Mexico? Our first step is to carefully examine the types of rock that make up the clasts in the Eocene river conglomerate in San Diego and then see if bedrock mountains of the same type can be found in Sonora. This search is made easier because a distinctive type of volcanic rock known as rhyolite dominates the Ballena Gravels (these rhyolite gravels are referred to as Poway rhyolites because of their abundant exposures south of the city of Poway). Rhyolite is especially rich in silicon, which means that in its magma state it was highly viscous. Rhyolite magma typically does not flow as lava but instead is blasted out by violent explosions after which mineral crystals and congealed rock fragments settle out, are deposited in layers, and harden into rock. These ancient rhyolitic rocks later were eroded and transported as gravels to San Diego, where they are ubiquitous; you can pick them up in many areas (see geologic maps in Kennedy and Peterson, 1975). The characteristics of the Poway rhyolite pebbles, cobbles, and boulders as described by Ron Kies are (1) commonly reddish-purplish, but some are gray; (2) very durable and hard to break with a hammer; (3) composed of 55–80% crystals (phenocrysts) separated by 20–45% very finely crystalline, dense, volcanic groundmass; and (4) always contain quartz crystals along with white- and salmon-colored feldspar crystals.

How can the Poway rhyolite gravels of San Diego be matched to volcanic bedrock in Sonora? In 1968 A. O. Woodford, E. E. Welday, and Richard Merriam analyzed the major-element chemistry of these rocks, and in 1972 John Minch made a regional comparison. These studies showed some similarities between the Poway rhyolite gravels and Sonoran bedrock, but they were not conclusive. More definitive tests were made by Terry Smith and me (1978, 1989) using statistical analyses of the trace-element chemistry of the rocks in order to uniquely "fingerprint" them. Statistical analyses were applied to rock concentrations of 16 elements (nickel, chromium, cobalt, vanadium, titanium, phosphorus, zirconium, yttrium, niobium, rubidium, strontium, barium, cesium, copper, zinc, manganese). These analyses yielded a strong correlation among Sonoran rhyolite bedrock, Poway rhyolite clasts in San Diego, and rhyolite clasts on Santa Cruz Island west of Los Angeles (Figure 5.15). Comparisons to other rhyolite bedrock localities and other Eocene conglomerates all failed to show a correlation, which strengthened the connection between Sonora and San Diego. (Santa Cruz Island will be discussed later.)

In science there can never be too much evidence. New tests are always emerging and they enable us to evaluate how well we know something or to form new hypotheses that better fit the growing pool of data. So, other types of analyses of Poway rhyolite clasts and Sonoran bedrock have been completed, for example,

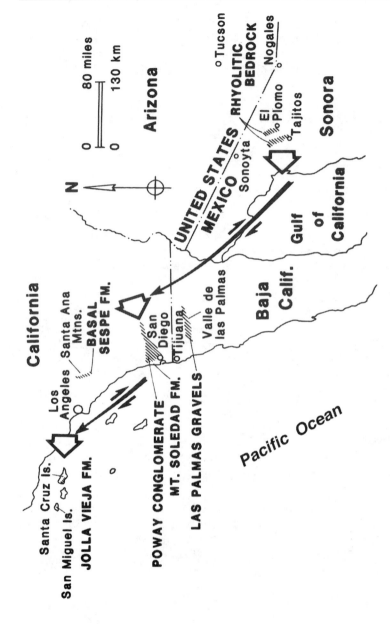

Figure 5.15. An integrated east-to-west Eocene depositional system.

1. Uranium/lead analyses were performed to measure the amounts of radioactive uranium and its decay product lead. Since the rate of decay of uranium to lead is known, measuring the amounts of uranium and lead in a rock allows us to determine when an igneous rock crystallized. Measurements by Jim Mattinson and Melissa Girty on Poway rhyolite clasts and Sonoran rhyolite bedrock place the crystallization age of the magma in Jurassic time, about 155 million years ago (Abbott and Smith, 1989).

2. Fission-track analysis measures the number of radioactive decay events that have damaged or scarred the atomic structure of a mineral crystal. Fission-track damage to crystals does not occur in minerals at great depth because at depth minerals are ductile due to the high temperatures. Crystal-lattice damage occurs only after the minerals/rocks are lifted toward the surface where they cool and become brittle. Thus, fission-track counts can date the time of mountain building or regional uplift. Roy Dokka examined the basement rocks in Sonora and determined that they were uplifted in Paleocene time, which means that they were elevated just in time for Eocene erosion and transportation of sedimentary debris.

3. The decay of the radioactive potassium isotope to argon gas also gives evidence of internal deformation and mountainous uplift. Potassium/argon analyses of Poway rhyolite gravels and Sonoran rhyolite bedrock by Dan Krummenacher testify to an uplift of Sonoran basement rock in Paleocene time (Abbott, Kies, Krummenacher, and Martin, 1983).

In Eocene time, before the Gulf of California existed, a large river eroded the Sonoran mountains, which uplifted in Paleocene time. The Sonoran mountains contain the distinctive rhyolite bedrock that originally solidified in Jurassic time. The Eocene Ballena river carried the rhyolite-gravel debris a long distance before dumping it as an alluvial fan on the San Diego coastal plain and offshore into a submarine canyon and submarine fan (Figure 5.16). At the same time two other large rivers tapped into different kinds of rhyolite bedrock: (1) To the north in Orange County are outcrops of conglomerate deposited from the Eocene Sespe river, which eroded a distinctive type of rhyolite bedrock known as Owl Creek rhyolite (Kies and Abbott, 1983). (2) In Baja California, 50 miles south of the Eocene Ballena river gravels in San Diego, lie outcrops of Eocene conglomerate deposited from the Eocene Las Palmas river (Figure 5.16), which eroded another distinctive type of rhyolite bedrock known as Las Palmas rhyolite.

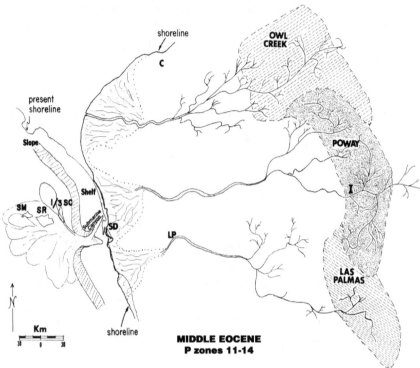

Figure 5.16. Paleogeographic map of San Diego (SD) region in middle Eocene time. The long-distance Ballena river brought coarse gravels to the Poway alluvial fan, which in turn funneled much sediment through a submarine canyon and out onto a submarine fan whose remains are now found on the northern Channel Islands. The islands (SM = San Miguel, SR = Santa Rosa, SC = Santa Cruz) are here placed in their Eocene positions. From Kies and Abbott, 1982.

FLOW CHARACTERISTICS OF THE EOCENE BALLENA RIVER

What did the Eocene Ballena river look like? Our first clue comes from examining the remaining masses of Ballena Gravels; they crop out discontinuously for over 16 miles in a west-southwest trend, exceed 360 feet in thickness, and reach 2 miles in width (Figure 5.13). The Ballena Gravels are found today in what was once an ancient valley cut by the Ballena river through the Peninsular Ranges. This 2-mile-wide valley was made by a big river!

Brad Steer undertook a quantitative study to describe the Eocene flow conditions. Variables measured in the field such as sediment-grain sizes, channel widths, and depths were combined with estimates of conditions in Eocene time such as channel-bottom slope, stream length, elevation of Sonoran source area, temperature, climate, and stream drainage-basin area. These values were plugged into multiple equations used to describe modern gravel-bed rivers (Steer and Abbott, 1984). Solving these equations gives us a picture of Eocene conditions where a long-distance (greater than 200 miles) river ran under a semiarid climate (Figure 4.4) with seasonally dominant rainfall of 20–30 inches per year and 100-year flood flows of about 90,000 cubic feet per second. Similar rivers today are the Nueces in Texas and several Argentine rivers flowing east from the Andes Mountains to the Atlantic Ocean.

The hypothesized semiarid climate with seasonal rainfall in later Eocene time is based on evidence gathered by Gary Peterson and me (1979) from Eocene sedimentary rocks locally: (1) the dominance in late Eocene rocks of conglomerate clasts produced by physical weathering and the relative scarcity of clay minerals produced by chemical weathering which requires abundant water; (2) the common presence of caliche, a calcium carbonate salt precipitated in sediments in climates where evaporation dominates over precipitation; (3) immature clay mineral varieties that form where water is scarce; and (4) gravel clasts fractured by salt-crystal growth, indicating that evaporation was dominant over precipitation.

Eocene Alluvial Fan System

When a flash flood on the Ballena river exited the mountains and flowed out onto the coastal plain it dumped much of its transported sediment onto a big alluvial fan (an apron-shaped body of coarse sediment). By looking at Figure 5.17, a beautiful physiographic diagram of San Diego drawn by E. H. Quayle in 1944, can you recognize the apex region of the Eocene alluvial fan? (Look in the upper left portion of the figure.) Alluvial fan growth stopped about 37 million years ago. Since then the Eocene alluvial fan has stood high while being eaten into by erosion. The remaining subaerial remnants of the alluvial fan have a volume calculated at 6.37 cubic miles (16.5 km^3) by Gary Simpson.

The Eocene alluvial fan and fan delta, along with the other Eocene depositional environments, are shown in Figure 5.12. Notice how the Ballena river built its alluvial fan across the coastal plain, burying the lagoon, tidal flat, beach, and marine shelf environments in the process. As the alluvial fan grew it spread directly into the ocean creating a fan delta that supplied a submarine canyon that in turn fed a deep-sea submarine fan.

The depositional systems ranging from river to alluvial fan to submarine canyon to submarine fan are all dominated by the distinctive Poway rhyolite clasts, and finding outcrops of these rocks is easy. The apex of the alluvial fan (Figure 5.18) is well exposed in the Nelson and Sloan quarry on Highway 67 north of Lakeside and immediately west of San Vicente Reservoir (*Thomas Guide,* p. 1211, H4). The main body of the alluvial fan is exposed along the north wall of Mission Valley (Figure 5.19, and *Thomas Guide,* p. 1249, E7). The Eocene submarine canyon fill is beautifully exposed in the beach cliffs north of Scripps Pier (Figure 5.20, and *Thomas Guide,* p. 1227, H3). The submarine fan is also well exposed in outcrops on the northern Channel Islands of San Miguel, Santa Rosa, and Santa Cruz (Figure 5.21).

The Poway rhyolite clast-bearing depositional environments combine to make a large, east-west oriented, integrated depositional system ranging from bedrock mountains in Sonora, Mexico, to Eocene river–alluvial fan–submarine canyon deposits in San Diego to a submarine fan now exposed in the northern Channel Islands. Two major offsets have separated this integrated depositional system since Eocene time (Figure 5.15): (1) on the Pacific Ocean floor, large-scale faulting has carried the Eocene submarine fan from San

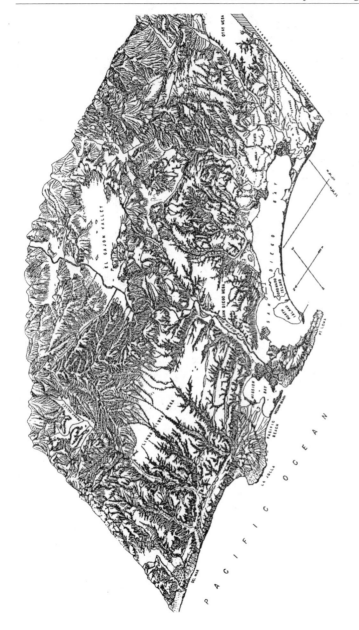

Figure 5.17. Physiographic diagram of San Diego drawn by E. H. Quayle, 1944.

Figure 5.18. Exposure of rocks in Nelson and Sloan quarry north of Lakeside. These conglomerates were deposited in the apex of the Eocene Poway alluvial fan. Note the extra-large clasts dropped when the Eocene river exited the mountains.

Figure 5.19. Eocene alluvial fan exposed on north wall of Mission Valley, west of Interstate 805.

Figure 5.20. Beach cliff exposures north of Scripps Pier showing sedimentary rocks that accumulated in the Eocene submarine canyon.

Figure 5.21. Santa Cruz Island exposures of sedimentary rocks deposited on the Eocene submarine fan offshore from San Diego.

103

Diego northward to the northern Channel Islands; and (2) the open-ing of the Gulf of California has drifted the San Diego area away from mainland Mexico.

Eocene Marine Field Trip: Beach Walk from Torrey Pines State Reserve to Scripps Pier

The 4.5-mile (7.3 km) walk along the beach from Torrey Pines State Reserve to Scripps Pier is an extraordinary experience, and thou-sands of geologists from all over the world have made this trek. The geologic story is better understood by walking from north to south (that is, from Torrey Pines State Reserve to Scripps Pier). A recom-mended strategy for a one-way trek is to have a companion park his or her car along La Jolla Shores Drive near Scripps Pier, then both of you drive in your car to the northern end of the beach cliffs at Torrey Pines State Reserve; park along North Torrey Pines Road (S21) (Figure 5.22, and *Thomas Guide,* p. 1207, G2). Begin by walk-ing south along the beach. Be sure to check the tide charts before beginning your walk—a low tide at the Scripps Pier end of the walk is desirable.

As you walk south from Torrey Pines to Scripps Pier you move upward through geologic time and experience the ancient changes in their original time sequence; you begin in older Eocene sedimen-tary rocks deposited in shallow water and pass into younger Eocene sedimentary rocks deposited in deeper marine water.

Refer to Figure 5.23, a schematic cross section of the beach cliffs prepared by Jeff May, and notice the three coccolith (yellow-green algae) fossil subzones indicated by the labels *R. inflata, D. strictus, and C. gigas* (the dotted lines on the diagram indicate where the subzones are separated from each other): (1) The subzone shown at the left of the diagram contains remains of *Rhabdosphaera inflata,* which lived about 49–48 million years ago; (2) the subzone shown near the middle of the diagram contains remains of *Discoaster stric-tus,* which lived about 48–47 million years ago; and (3) the subzone shown at the far right of the diagram contains *Chiasmolithus gi-gas,* which lived about 47–46.5 million years ago. In other words, as you walk a horizontal path along the beach from north to south, you

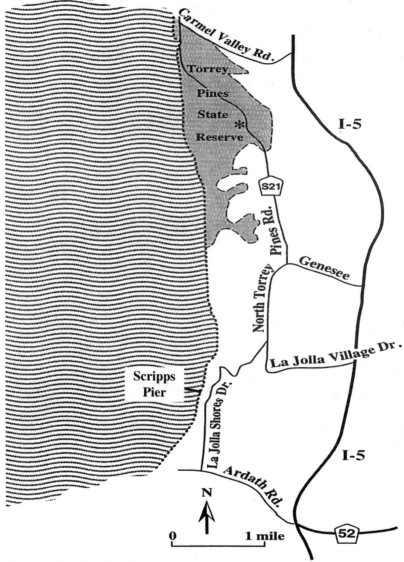

Figure 5.22. Map for Eocene marine field trip: Beach walk from Torrey Pines State Reserve to Scripps Pier.

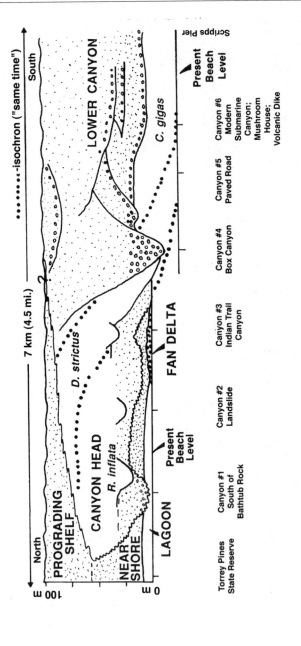

Figure 5.23. Schematic cross section showing age relationships within the Eocene submarine canyon exposed in beach cliffs between Torrey Pines State Reserve (north end) and Scripps Pier (south end). From May, Lohmar, Warme, and Morgan, 1991.

walk a younging-upward course through the prehistoric rock and fossil record.

BEACH WALK, FIRST SEGMENT

The first mile of the walk takes you along the cliffs in Torrey Pines State Reserve through Eocene sedimentary rocks that were deposited in shallow marine water. Near the base of the cliffs are greenish mudstone beds of the lagoonal Delmar Formation. They alternate with and are overlain by the orangish sandstones of the coastal tidal-flat deposits of the Torrey Formation. If seaward tidal-flat deposits (Torrey Sandstone) lie on top of landward lagoonal sedimentary rocks (Delmar Formation), was Eocene sea level rising or falling? Stop and consider this question in three dimensions (try using your hands to model the scenario). What you will come up with is that during middle Eocene time, the sea level rose (Figure 5.3).

As you look at the greenish mudstone of the Delmar Formation, notice the following:

- Brackish-water oyster and snail fossils (remember that you are in the protected Torrey Pines State Reserve, so look at and photograph the fossils but please do *not* collect them).
- Carbonized wood fragments often colored with bright yellow where modern-day groundwater is leaching sulphur from this Eocene wood.
- Trace fossils of grazing, churning, and domiciling Eocene invertebrate organisms (Figure 5.24).

As you walk farther down the beach notice that the orangish sandstone layers are now more visible. Notice the following features:

- Sandstones deposited on top of asymmetric U-shaped bases (channel bottoms) that were eroded into mudstone and later filled with sands deposited in a tidal channel.
- Cross laminations (cross bedding) inclined with variable directions that tell of shifting channels and alternating flood- and ebb-tide flows.

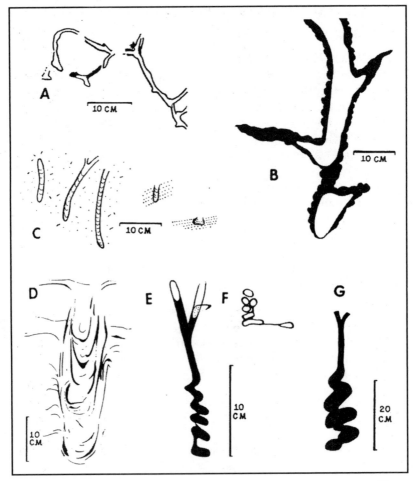

Figure 5.24. Trace fossils from Delmar and Torrey Formations. From Boyer and Warme, 1975.

- Alternating light- and dark-colored cross beds showing the daily record of high and low tides; light-colored quartz and feldspar grains settled out of stronger flood tides, and dark-colored biotite flakes settled out of weaker ebb tides.

- Beautiful, orange banding patterns (*liesegang bands*); the coloring is caused by minerals in the sandstone interacting with and becoming oxidized by geologically recent, oxygen-rich groundwaters.

BATHTUB ROCK

Bathtub Rock (rather boringly renamed Flat Rock by the California Park Service) is a resistant slab of Delmar Formation that juts into the ocean as a low-relief headland (Figure 5.25). Climb onto Bathtub Rock and examine the bathtub, which is a partially sand-filled shaft reputedly dug long ago in hopes of locating coal deposits that would influence the decision to locate the transcontinental railroad in San Diego rather than in Los Angeles. As you look around in the Bathtub Rock area, notice the following:

Figure 5.25. Aerial view of Bathtub Rock, Torrey Pines State Beach.

- A marked erosion surface within the Delmar Formation that is used as a foot path (Figure 5.26). Three of the people in Figure 5.26 are standing on horizontally layered lagoonal sedimentary rocks that were truncated by erosion to create a little hill in

Eocene time. This was followed by deposition of lagoonal sediments against the side of the hill and, as time went on, above the hill. Note how the upper sediment layers appear "draped" over the exposure-hardened hill. These rock layers were deposited as horizontal sheets. They became inclined (acquired their dip) after the water-saturated soft sediments were buried and compacted beneath overlying sediments that caused their pore water to be squeezed out.

- Look higher up the cliff face to see a conglomerate made largely of mudstone pebbles, cobbles, and boulders. On the south side of Bathtub Rock the clay-clast conglomerate rests on a south-sloping erosion surface that comes down to beach level (Figure 5.27). This erosion surface is part of the northern wall of a *large* Eocene submarine canyon. Look carefully at Figure 5.28 and notice the geologic details of the beach cliff south of Bathtub

Figure 5.26. View south of beach cliff on north side of Bathtub Rock. Three people are standing on an erosion surface within the Delmar Formation.

Rock. Figure 5.28a shows the erosion surface cut across the shallow-water deposits of the Delmar and Torrey Formations. Figure 5.28b is a sketch of the submarine-canyon sediments deposited on top of the erosion surface.

Figure 5.27. View south of beach cliff south of Bathtub Rock. Erosion surface at base of Eocene submarine canyon slopes from left to right (north to south) about halfway up cliff.

Look for the following features within the submarine-canyon sedimentary rocks:

- Multiple erosion surfaces.
- Pieces of mudstone ripped up during canyon erosion and redeposited as clasts.
- Some undercut and redeposited sedimentary blocks the size of automobiles.
- Convoluted, thin layers of sediment deformed by Eocene pore water that escaped upwards during and shortly after deposition.

•   Other sedimentary features such as cut-and-fill channels, graded bedding, ripple laminations, burrowing, planar laminae, and flame structures.

You will walk another 3.5 miles (5.5 km) to Scripps Pier, but you will not reach the south wall of the submarine canyon—the Eocene submarine canyon was big! It is for the experience of walking through a submarine canyon that geologists from throughout the world come here to look at these beach cliffs cut across a sediment-filled Eocene submarine canyon.

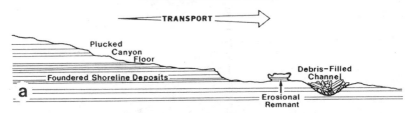

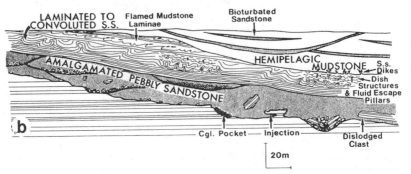

Figure 5.28. Cross-sectional sketches at Bathtub Rock looking landward (east). (a) Sketch of erosion surface cut at base of submarine canyon south from Bathtub Rock; (b) characteristics of sedimentary fill of submarine canyon south from Bathtub Rock. Drawings by Jeff May.

TORREY PINES LANDSLIDE

As you continue walking down the beach from Bathtub Rock, you will walk past Canyon 2 (Figure 5.23); notice the massive landslide south of this canyon. The area of chaparral vegetation now almost at beach level formerly grew on the terrace surface on top of the cliff; the land has been lowered slowly by the combined actions of gravity-pulled landslides and ocean-wave erosion at the toe of the landslide. Where has the main mass of the landslide gone? Ocean waves have eroded and redistributed the landslide sediments southward, creating the especially wide sandy beach you will walk on as you continue south. As you stroll southward, look up at the beach cliffs and notice the cross-cutting erosion surfaces that formed as channels about 2,000 feet (600 meters) across that were later filled with sediments about 250 feet (75 meters) thick. Each channel was active at a different time in the history of the submarine canyon. To visualize these channels in action during Eocene time, imagine that each submarine-canyon channel is like the active channel in a modern river valley; the channel carries water for a time but is then abandoned and filled with sediment as a new channel forms somewhere else in the river valley.

INDIAN TRAIL CANYON

At the mouth of Indian Trail Canyon (Canyon 3 on Figure 5.23), the oldest rocks in the beach cliffs are exposed—heavily weathered Mount Soledad Formation conglomerate overlain by the early Eocene-age, kaolinite-rich tropical soil shown in Figure 4.3. On top of the paleosol (ancient tropical soil) is a thick mass of sandstone that was deposited in a middle Eocene channel inside the submarine canyon. Pause and consider the sequence of events here: a tropical soil is overlain by sands deposited in a submarine canyon. Many things must have happened in the interval of time between the formation of these two very different materials (soil and submarine canyon sands). But the record of those intervening events is not preserved in the rocks because Eocene erosion destroyed them, leaving only an unconformity.

As you continue walking southward, notice the continued presence of Eocene-age, large cross-cutting channels within the beach cliffs. South of the hang-glider port, as conglomerates begin to appear in the beach cliffs, notice the large active landslide pulling away from the cliffs. At 9:00 a.m. on 29 January 1982, a mass broke loose (1.8 million cubic yards) from the cliffs and hit the beach in two distinct thuds strong enough to be recorded on a seismograph. The landslide mass spilled into the ocean, completely blocking the beach. Many questions can be asked about this event—for example, (1) what has happened to this mass of sediment since 1982? (2) was the slide mass removed by nature or by humans? (3) how was the slide mass removed to reopen the beach? (4) is the landslide mass now stable? (5) what times of year present the most danger for additional movement? Answers to questions 1, 2, and 3: Ocean waves efficiently eroded the sandy landslide mass and pushed the sand southward as longshore-drifted beach sand. Unfortunately, most of this beach sand has since been "lost" as it poured into a modern submarine canyon, which funneled the sand into deep ocean water, thus removing it from the beaches for at least millions of years. Answers to questions 4 and 5: the mass is not stable; it will continue moving. Beach cliff failures occur most frequently during the winter when the beach sandmass is minimal and the larger ocean waves of winter beat against the base of the cliff. (For further information on the landslide, see Vanderhurst, McCarthy, and Hannan, 1982.)

BOX CANYON

Box Canyon (Canyon 4 on Figure 5.23) cuts through a beautiful, sediment-filled Eocene channel (Figure 5.29). The channel is 4,000 feet (1,200 m) wide and 250 feet (75 m) thick; it contains Poway rhyolite-bearing conglomerate at its base, which is overlain by sandstone, which in turn is overlain by gray mudstone—a classic fining upwards of sediment-grain sizes within a filled channel. Notice the convoluted and slumped gray mudstone below and south of this channel.

Continuing southward, the amount of Eocene conglomerate in the beach cliffs continues to increase. Now is probably a good time to stop and consider the Eocene submarine canyon in a 3-dimensional and 4-dimensional context. So far you have walked about 2.5

Figure 5.29. Box Canyon eroded through an Eocene submarine channel (4,000 feet wide) filled, in sequence, by gravel–sand–mud.

miles across the submarine canyon (with another 0.75 mile to go). Remember from Figure 5.23 that the Eocene sedimentary fill becomes younger as you move southward. Remember also that the most common sediment size filling the submarine canyon on its northern, older side was fine-grained mudstone that gave way southward to sandstone as the canyon fill became younger, and now you are looking at abundant conglomerate, which dominates the cliffs all the way to Scripps Institution of Oceanography. What is going on here? The sediment fill in the Eocene submarine canyon is coarsening as we move south; that is, you are walking up the sedimentary sequence and moving upward through geologic time. What does this tell us? The massive Poway alluvial fan and fan delta (Figure 5.12) was prograding (advancing seaward), bringing ever-coarser sediments into the ocean.

As you approach the "mushroom" house on the beach, notice how the amount of beach sand decreases markedly and is effectively gone just south of the mushroom house at the rocky beach cliff. What happened to the beach sand? Canyon 6 on Figure 5.23, just north of the mushroom house, is actually an active submarine canyon. The modern beach sand is pushed southward by incoming waves. When sand reaches the submarine canyon, it spills into the canyon and flows westward under the pull of gravity into the deep ocean. If you look seaward from this canyon, you may see dive boats anchored close to shore; and there may be SCUBA divers in the water looking into the steep-walled head of the modern submarine canyon. Consider this: The modern submarine canyon is eroded into the sediment fill of an Eocene submarine canyon. From a philosophical perspective, the canyon is telling us that the more things change, the more they seem the same.

MIOCENE VOLCANIC DIKE

Walking south past the mushroom house and onto the rocks, notice the in-place volcanic rock trending along a line from lands' edge into the surf zone heading toward Scripps Pier. This rock formed from magma filling a fracture and then solidifying to form this dike in Miocene time, about 14 million years ago.

MARINE WILDLIFE REFUGE

You near the end of this stroll as you move along the base of the conglomerate-dominated sea cliffs. These submarine-canyon conglomerates were once gravels moving downslope toward the submarine fan sitting in deeper water to the west; but their journey stopped, and they were deposited en route in the Eocene submarine canyon. Some gravity-caused sedimentary features can be seen on close inspection of the flat rock area jutting out onto the beach. Figure 5.30 shows complexly folded, deep-marine mudstone layers pulled downslope by gravity with much resultant crumpling and folding. Figure 5.31 is a clay-pebble conglomerate formed where the downslope pull of gravity was so overpowering that the mud layers broke apart into pieces.

Figure 5.30. Mudstone layers in lower submarine canyon distorted by gravity-induced sliding.

Figure 5.31. Mud clasts formed by breakup of mud layer pulled downslope by gravity.

117

CHAPTER 6
OLIGOCENE HISTORY

As 19th-century geologists continued studying Cenozoic rocks and fossils, new subdivisions of the fossil record were defined. In 1854 Heinrich von Beyrich examined the fossiliferous strata in northern Germany and Belgium and recognized the fossils as younger than the Eocene of Paris. He named this interval the Oligocene. Today, we recognize Oligocene time as having occurred 33.7 to 23.8 million years ago.

The presence of Oligocene rocks was not recognized in the San Diego region until 1985 when grading began for the EastLake development in eastern Chula Vista. Construction-related earth moving uncovered fossils of a diverse and abundant vertebrate fauna, and these were collected by paleontologists affiliated with the San Diego Museum of Natural History (Deméré, 1986).

Tectonics
During Oligocene time, the westerly movement of the North American plate caused it to collide with segments of the spreading center in the eastern Pacific Ocean (Figure 6.1). The initial collision occurred about 29 million years ago, around the middle of Oligocene time, and involved southern California. The collision marked the beginning of the change from subduction of oceanic plate (Farallon plate) beneath southern California to the large-scale horizontal

faulting that still continues. Today, the earthquakes we experience remind us that the western Californias are cut by faults that typically have their western side moving northward, that is, right-lateral, strike-slip faults.

The switch from subduction to horizontal or strike-slip faulting with major offsets was also marked by some volcanism. San Diego has no known Oligocene volcanoes or hardened lava flows, but it has considerable volumes of volcanic ash that rained down from the skies. Where are the volcanoes or volcanic vents that emitted the ash? We do not yet know. Three candidates are volcanic plugs in northwestern San Diego County: (1) Cerro de la Calavera in northeastern Carlsbad, (2) Morro Hill in the northern tip of Oceanside, and (3) near Horno Summit on Camp Pendleton. None of these volcanic plugs has yet been dated. One of these might have been active in Oligocene time, or perhaps none of them were.

As the North American plate neared the spreading center in the Pacific Ocean (Figure 6.1), it was running over increasingly younger, warmer, more buoyant oceanic crust; this caused a regional uplift and fracturing of the North American continental margin. As the San Diego region was uplifted, the ocean shoreline was forced to retreat to the west. The uplifted land was eroded, shedding coarse-grained gravels and sands that accumulated locally in nonmarine basins; in other words, coarse sediments began filling in nearby topographic low spots. At the same time, volcanic ash was settling down from the atmosphere and being deposited in layers.

All in all, Eocene time in San Diego was significantly different from Oligocene time. During Eocene time, the oceanic plate was subducting eastward at a shallow angle (Figure 5.1), causing a mountainous uplift in Arizona and Sonora, Mexico. An Eocene river running from mountains in Sonora brought exotic gravels to San Diego that accumulated in a large alluvial fan that dominated the local landscape (Figure 5.12). But tectonic events late in Eocene time cut off the long-distance Eocene Ballena river. Oligocene time found San Diego with local streams eroding local hills and depositing relatively small volumes of sediment in local basins. In effect, the grand-scale Eocene topography of the San Diego region was being cannibalized to provide local sediments during Oligocene time.

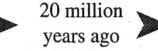

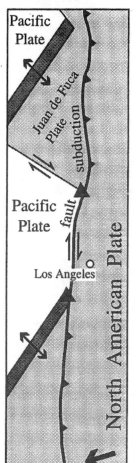

Figure 6.1. Early in Oligocene time, the Farallon oceanic plate was subducting beneath the Californias, and the Pacific plate was moving northwest toward Japan. In mid-Oligocene time, about 29 million years ago, North America ran into part of the Pacific Ocean spreading center; thus uplifting the continental edge. In early Miocene time, about 20 million years ago, major horizontal-displacement faulting was underway.

Meanwhile, the ever-evolving biologic world produced a very different set of animals that lived here under cooler climatic conditions.

Oligocene and younger rocks in San Diego are thicker and more voluminous in the southern end of the region. Bill Elliott made gravity surveys of San Diego and showed that the land area from Interstate 8 south to the Mexican border has sunk progressively downward to a depth of a mile near the international border. This sinking basin has been kept nearly full of sediments through time due to deliveries from running water and the pull of gravity.

Oligocene Climate

The world witnessed a long-term shift in climatic regime during Eocene time. When the Eocene dawned about 55 million years ago, Earth was at the height of a "Torrid Age" with the hottest climate of Cenozoic time. But during Eocene time, the global climate began a cooling trend, which led to the formation of major ice sheets on Antarctica at the beginning of Oligocene time 33.7 million years ago. The Oligocene rock and fossil records are marked by this cooling trend, which has persisted for over 30 million years and led to the great Ice Age of the last 2.67 million years—an Ice Age that continues today.

Oligocene Formations

The Oligocene strata in San Diego have no officially defined names that follow the rules of the North American Commission on Stratigraphic Nomenclature. The best discussion of late Eocene and Oligocene formation names is found in a 1991 paper by Steve Walsh and Tom Deméré. They refer to the Oligocene rocks as the Otay formation (Figure 1.7).

OLIGOCENE AGE

The Oligocene age is well defined. First, the abundant land-mammal fossils correlate with the early Arikareean, a North American Land Mammal Age (NALMA) that lasted from about 30 to 24 million years ago. Moreover, the San Diego mammal fossils seem to be from the earliest part of this NALMA interval, 30–27 million years ago. Second, one of the volcanic ash layers was collected by Dick Berry, who arranged for an argon-40/argon-39 radiometric analysis by J. D. Obradovich that yielded an age of 28.86 million years (Berry, 1991). Third, the magnetic polarity of the Oligocene fossil-rich sedimentary rock layers was measured by Don Prothero (1991). He found that the rocks all have reverse polarity (a south magnetic pole) that correlates with Chron 10R, which occurred 29.1–28.4 million years ago (see Chapter 1 for discussion of the magnetic polarity–reversal time scale).

BENTONITE

Some of the volcanic ash layers were altered chemically after deposition to form bentonite, a generalized group of clay minerals. Bentonites have a range of properties, but typically they are white, cream, or pale pink in color, have a waxy or soapy feel, and commonly expand greatly when exposed to water. Soils developed on bentonite can usually be recognized by the "popcorn" texture that forms when the bentonite expands on wetting and shrinks on drying (Figure 6.2).

The Otay bentonite was first described in 1890 and first mined in 1917. In the following four decades about 83,000 tons of bentonite were mined by various operators. Scars left by mining are still visible as horizontal ledges high on the south wall of the Otay River valley about 1–2 miles east of Interstate 805. The bentonite was used principally for its adsorbing ability. The oil industry used it to clean heavy oils, kerosene, and gasoline and as an oil-well drilling mud. The Otay bentonite has also been used as a filler in paint and in water softening. Although reserves of high-grade bentonite in the Otay River valley area were estimated at 8.5 million tons by Cleveland (1960), the Otay River valley land is now more valuable for urban developments such as the White Water Canyon Amusement Park and the 20,000-seat Coors outdoor amphitheater.

Oligocene Vertebrate Fossils

Eastern Chula Vista holds a bonanza of Oligocene vertebrate fossils that began to be discovered in 1985. Why did it take so long for the fossils to be found? At and close to the surface the bentonitic

Figure 6.2. Bentonite with "popcorn" weathering, at intersection of Otay Valley Road and lower Heritage Road. Car keys for scale.

clays of the Otay formation expand and contract so much that they break up fossils into tiny fragments. How were they finally found? By paleontologists searching through some 7 million cubic yards of rock that had been ripped up and broken apart by bulldozers and graders during the initial phases of the EastLake development. Thanks to Tom Deméré, Richard Cerutti, Brad Riney, Mark Roeder, Bob Gutzler, Steve Walsh, Don Swanson, Paul Majors, Nancy Cox, and Pablo Lopez, we now have thousands of fossils from 24 Oligocene species—2 bird species, 4 reptile species, and 18 mammal species. The most abundant fossils are oreodonts, pig-like hoofed mammals distantly related to camels; oreodonts went extinct 5 million years ago (Figures 6.3 and 6.4).

What did the San Diego area look like 29 million years ago? There were rolling hills cut by small streams, and the region was occasionally dusted by layers of volcanic ash. The coastal hills and slopes were grazed by gregarious herds of oreodonts and other extinct animals, some of whom have related species living today. The

Figure 6.3. Skull, lower jaw, and gnawed forelimb of the domestic goat-sized oreodont Mesoreodon. Scale is 1 cm per division. Collected by Brad Riney (San Diego Society of Natural History specimen 28225).

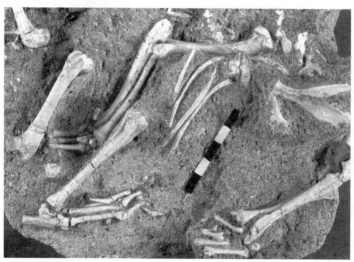

Figure 6.4. Articulated forelimbs and hindlimbs of domestic cat-sized oreodont Sespia. Scale is 1 cm per division. Collected by Brad Riney (SDSNH specimen 31314).

slopes were home to relatively small and slender rhinoceros and small, llama-like camels. Rhinoceros were common in North America until 18 million years ago, and camels lived in southern California until a mere 10,000 years ago. In Oligocene San Diego there were mice (Figure 6.5), shrews, hedgehogs, gophers, rabbits, and mouse deer (chevrotain) that were preyed upon by fox-like and short-faced dogs and saber-tooth carnivores (Figure 6.6). Also on the ground were lizards and tortoise. You can see these Oligocene fossils at the San Diego Museum of Natural History in Balboa Park.

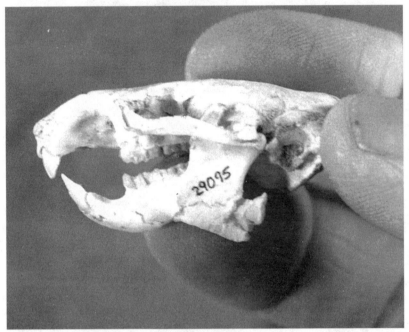

Figure 6.5. Skull and lower jaws of the extinct rodent Meniscomys. *Collected by Richard Cerutti (SDSNH specimen 29095).*

Oligocene Field Trip: Otay Valley Road

Geologic field work often takes us to places of exceptional beauty. So far, the study of San Diego geology has taken us down Los Peñasquitos Canyon, to the tidepools on Point Loma, and along the

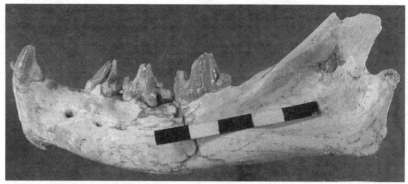

Figure 6.6. Lower jaw of the false saber-tooth carnivore Nimravus. *Scale is 1 cm per division. Collected by Richard Cerutti (SDSNH specimen 31242).*

beach cliffs at Torrey Pines and La Jolla. On the other hand, there are times when we work in less spectacular areas, such as during the study of the Oligocene rocks. This trip provides a close-up view of the roadcuts along Otay Valley Road as it climbs southward up-grade toward auto heaven, the prolific yards of wrecked autos on the mesa (Figure 6.7; and *Thomas Guide,* p. 1331, B6 and C7). The road is narrow, lined with "no parking" signs, littered with automobile debris and other rubbish, and frequented by fast and vocal drivers. But for the serious student of Oligocene rocks in San Diego, there is no better place to visit. If nothing else, drive slowly along the road and eyeball the outcrops. If you make only one stop, it probably should be to collect bentonite. Turn east on lower Heritage Road, park immediately, and dig into the roadcut by the stop sign to uncover thin layers of the unique, cream-pink colored, waxy–soapy bentonite (Figures 6.7 and 6.8).

The exposed Oligocene sequence of sedimentary rocks is about 260 feet (79 m) thick. The sediment sizes fine upward from gritstone at the base to finer sandstone and mudstone above; higher up the grade, volcanic ash is found.

OTAY FORMATION GRITSTONE STOP
Roadcuts near the bottom of the grade expose a 70-foot thick interval characterized by coarse- and very coarse-grained sandstone with

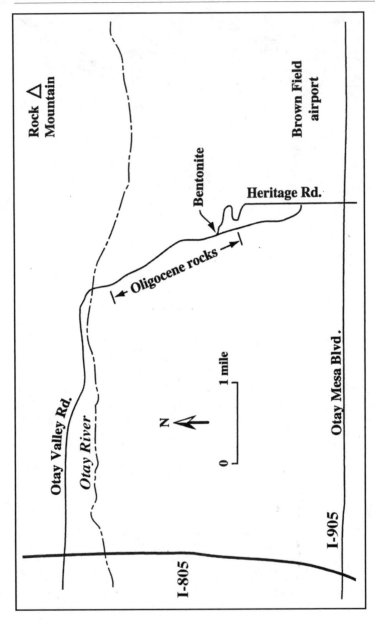

Figure 6.7. Location of Oligocene rock exposures in roadcuts on east side of Otay Valley Road.

Figure 6.8. Layers of light-colored sandstone and darker mudstone in the Otay formation at intersection of Otay Valley and lower Heritage Roads. Digging into the bottom few feet of rock layers in the roadcut near the stop sign will uncover thin layers of bentonite.

abundant angular granules and small pebbles; geologists informally call this sediment mixture a gritstone. Walk over and look closely at these rocks (be careful of traffic), and consider the following:

- What is the composition of the gritstone? The sediment is dominated by coarse grains of quartz, feldspar, and plutonic- and volcanic-rock fragments.
- What were the sources of the pebbles? The pebbles are composed of plutonic and volcanic rocks that look similar to hills of basement rocks immediately to the east. The volcanic-rock clasts look like the early Cretaceous Santiago Peak Volcanics now being mined at Rock Mountain, just a stone's throw away in the Otay River valley.

- How far did these sediments travel before being deposited? Notice the sharp angular surfaces on many of the pebbles, granules, and very coarse sand grains; they testify to a short distance of travel. The farther a pebble or coarse sand grain rolls downstream, the smoother and rounder it becomes.
- Notice that the sedimentary rock layers are tabular and laterally continuous as opposed to containing numerous U-shaped channels. Also note that coarser-grained beds are overlain by finer-grained beds in stacked, fining-upward sequences. In what environment did the sedimentary rocks accumulate? Probably in sand-filled stream valleys.

OTAY FORMATION SANDSTONE-MUDSTONE STOP

Moving up the grade, the grain sizes of the sedimentary rocks, in general, become finer. Mudstone beds appear in the section, and more of the sandstone beds have finer grain sizes than those below (Figure 6.9). The sandstone-mudstone unit is about 190 feet (58 m) thick. Notice the following:

- Sedimentary layers are organized in fining-upward packages with pebbly coarse-grained sandstone overlain by progressively finer grain-sized beds. These grain-size trends represent filling of broad stream channels.
- Mudstone beds are common. They represent stream overbank sedimentation or filling of abandoned channels. These layers hold the most vertebrate fossils.
- Bentonite layers can be found in the mudstone beds. Dig into popcorn-textured beds (Figure 6.2) and search for creamy-pinkish, waxy-soapy layers a few inches thick.

PLIOCENE SAN DIEGO FORMATION

About 50 feet below the auto junkyards lies the unconformity eroded on top of the Otay formation. Above the erosion surface lie the loosely consolidated sands of the San Diego Formation with its distinctive "badlands" weathering style (Figure 6.10). The San Diego Formation here is about 35 feet (11 m) thick; it was deposited in nearshore, shallow marine water. A significant site is the contact

Figure 6.9. Beds of Oligocene sandstone and mudstone containing volcanic ash exposed along Otay Valley Road south of the Otay River.

between the Oligocene Otay and Pliocene San Diego formations (Figure 6.11). The contact is an unconformity with 27 million years of rocks and fossils missing. Find the erosion surface in the roadcut and see the large sand-filled boreholes (Figure 6.12). The large holes were bored by pholad clams into the eroded Otay formation exposed on the Pliocene sea floor.

Figure 6.10. Pliocene San Diego Formation sandstone in roadcut on upper Otay Valley Road below auto junkyards. Notice the distinctive "badlands" weathering style in the loosely bound sandstone and the thin horizontal beds of gravel deposited near the Pliocene shoreline.

Opposite page:

Figure 6.11. Contact between the Pliocene San Diego Formation and the Oligocene Otay formation. This contact, which is shown at waist level of students, is an unconformity with about 27 million years of geologic time unrepresented by rocks or fossils.

Figure 6.12. Close-up view of contact between San Diego Formation and Otay formation. Notice the large sand-filled boreholes made by rock-boring pholad clams (Family Pholadidae). These Pliocene clams bored into the hardened Oligocene sandy mudstone on the exposed sea floor.

Figure 6.11

Figure 6.12

133

CHAPTER 7
MIOCENE HISTORY

The Miocene was defined by Charles Lyell after studying fossils near Bordeaux, France; around Vienna, Austria; and near Turin, Italy. He detailed the results of this study in the 3rd edition of his book *Principles of Geology,* which was published in 1833. Lyell subdivided Tertiary rocks into units of different ages "based on the comparative proportion of living species found as fossils in each." Lyell described the Miocene as having about 18% of its fossil species found as living species today. We now define Miocene time as having occurred 23.8 to 5.3 million years ago.

Miocene rocks are rare in the City of San Diego but are found in abundance (1) within the Salton Trough to the east, (2) from Oceanside to Laguna Beach and farther north, and (3) from Tijuana and farther south, including the Coronado Islands.

Salton Trough

Southeastern California is dominated by the low-elevation Colorado Desert. Its most pronounced feature is the Salton Trough, an elongate tectonic depression that extends from near Palm Springs to the head of the Gulf of California. The Salton Trough is essentially the northern end of the Gulf of California; however, the Colorado River delta has built sideways across the trough, forming a dam that blocks the Gulf of California seawater from flowing north. The land of the Salton Trough has been pulled apart. This extension has caused rocks of many different ages to rise to the surface, allowing us to inspect them.

The rocks exposed in the Salton Trough testify to a long and complex geologic history. The oldest rocks are known because Rick Miller identified Ordovician conodont fossils in limestone (marble) exposed in the Coyote Mountains just north of Ocotillo in western Imperial County. Through Paleozoic and Triassic time, the region lay beneath the sea on the western margin of the continent. Jurassic time was dominated by magmatism that reached its peak in mid-Cretaceous time with the formation of the voluminous plutonic rocks of the Peninsular Ranges. When the formation and intrusion of magma stopped, the agents of erosion took over with a vengeance, reducing the mountains to a broad erosion plain by Eocene time. The long-distance Ballena river of Eocene time fed sediments to the massive Poway alluvial fan in San Diego until it was cut off 37 million years ago (+/- 2 million years) by geologic events to the east. Apparently the land had begun extending, and as the topography pulled apart it disrupted the Ballena river, thus sending its water elsewhere.

The rate of extension increased markedly in Miocene time, resulting in the initial formation of the Salton Trough as a major pull-apart basin bounded by faults (Figure 7.1). In 1996 Eric Frost worked out a sequence of events that are remarkable for their mind-boggling scale. The stretching apart of the region resulted in entire mountains detaching from the rocks below and sliding with near-horizontal movements, albeit at the slow rates of geologic processes. For example, in Anza-Borrego Desert State Park about 24 million years ago, stretching resulted in basal detachment that sent the Vallecito Mountains (upper plate) sliding southeast off the Yaqui Ridge area (lower plate) (Figure 7.2). In turn, the Fish Creek Mountains (upper plate) slid southeast off the top of the Vallecito Mountains (then a lower plate). This sliding-apart process mostly stopped about 12 million years ago, leaving a deep hole in the area between the Vallecito and Fish Creek Mountains called the Fish Creek–Vallecito basin (Figure 7.1). During the next several million years the basin filled with sediments thousands of feet thick.

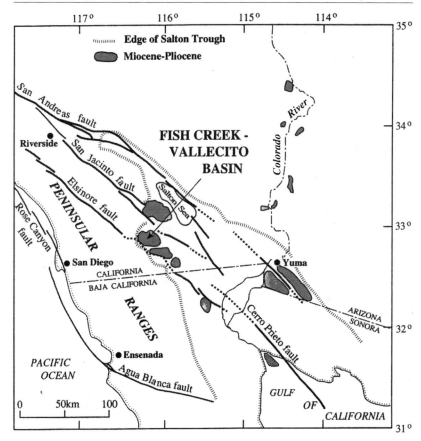

Figure 7.1. Map of northernmost Gulf of California and Salton Trough. Sedimentary rocks in the Fish Creek–Vallecito basin are beautifully exposed in Split Mountain Gorge.

The Gulf of California began forming in middle Miocene time, about 14–13 million years ago. It originally was a long, relatively narrow basin, with some ocean water flooding by 13 million years ago as shown by marine clam and snail fossils on Isla Tiburon identified by Judy Terry Smith. In middle Miocene time, the Anza-Borrego region and San Diego lay to the south, alongside the present-

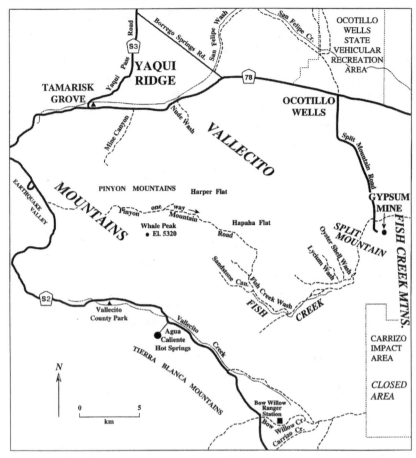

Figure 7.2. Map showing Yaqui Ridge, Vallecito Mountains, Split Mountain, and Fish Creek Mountains.

day state of Sonora, Mexico. The area was then a narrow rift basin accumulating sediments. During the time from about 13 to 5.5 million years ago, Baja California and southern California were part of the North American tectonic plate. Around 5.5 million years ago the sea-floor spreading process improved in efficiency and the Californias were transferred to the Pacific tectonic plate. For the last 5.5 million years, the Gulf of California has opened at about 2.3 inches (6 cm) per year to create the still-youthful ocean basin shape it displays today.

An excellent view of some rocks that record part of this complex geologic history may be seen by driving up Fish Creek Wash through Split Mountain Gorge in Anza-Borrego Desert State Park (Figure 7.2; and *Thomas Guide,* p. 410, F1). Several stops afford beautiful and instructive views of the area (Figure 7.3).

Miocene Field Trip: Fish Creek Wash Through Split Mountain Gorge in Anza-Borrego Desert State Park

The rocks of Split Mountain Gorge have been exposed by events beginning 0.9 million years ago when squeezing at bends in the Elsinore fault zone caused Miocene and Pliocene sedimentary strata in the Fish Creek–Vallecito basin to be uplifted and folded to create Split Mountain. The Split Mountain area has been folded into a northwest-trending, broad anticline (uparch). Later, the area was cut by a small-scale, north-trending, horizontal-displacement fault zone whose west side moved to the south. Fish Creek has eroded a gorge largely along the fault zone, creating beautiful cross-section views of the Miocene and Pliocene sediments that poured into the former basin between the Vallecito and Fish Creek Mountains.

The easiest way to drive this route is south from Ocotillo Wells on Split Mountain Road (Figure 7.2). When you reach Fish Creek, just before the road ends at the gypsum quarry, turn right onto the stream bed. The bed of Fish Creek is the "road" used to drive through Split Mountain Gorge (Figure 7.3).

STOP 1: FISH CREEK WASH–PARK ENTRANCE OVERVIEW

Drive up Fish Creek for a mile or so, then stop your car, get out, and look to the south. Sweep your eyes across the topographic and geologic setting. To the west, on your right, rises the steep face of the plutonic-rock dominated Vallecito Mountains. In Eric Frost's reconstruction of the events in the Salton Trough, the Vallecito Mountains slid eastward to about their present position during Miocene

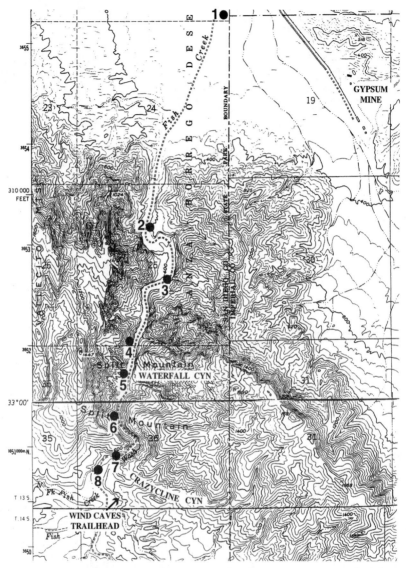

Figure 7.3. Map for Split Mountain Gorge field trip showing numbered stops described in text.

time; the major movement began about 24 million years ago, peaked about 18 million years ago, and slowed as the mountains reached their present position about 12 million years ago.

Now look to the southeast, your left, over the gypsum quarry to the mixed plutonic and metamorphic rocks of the Fish Creek Mountains. In Eric Frost's interpretation, the Fish Creek Mountains (upper plate) formerly sat on top of the Vallecito Mountains (lower plate) before taking a Miocene journey to the east.

Between the two plutonic rock highlands lies the Fish Creek-Vallecito basin that received varied sediments from about 14 to 1 million years ago. Thanks to faulting in the last million years, the sediments that filled this basin have been uplifted to form Split Mountain. Looking south-southwest, you can see the mouth of Split Mountain Gorge cut by Fish Creek through Split Mountain (Figure 7.4). The rugged cliffs of conglomerate on the west side are Miocene

Figure 7.4. View south up Fish Creek Wash to mouth of Split Mountain Gorge. Cliff is composed of Miocene alluvial-fan sedimentary rocks.

alluvial-fan sediments shed from the steep, east-facing front of the Vallecito Mountains. Looking at the east side of Split Mountain Gorge (Figure 7.5) you can see the southern skyline capped by the steep cliffs of the quartz-cemented Split Mountain sturzstrom deposit; it moved at ultra-high velocity from the Vallecito Mountains in latest Miocene time. Farther east lies the impressive quarry where the U.S. Gypsum Company mines nearly pure gypsum. The mining operation owns its own narrow-gauge railroad to transport gypsum south to Plaster City located next to Interstate 8 and the San Diego and Arizona Eastern Railroad. You are looking at the largest operating gypsum mine in the United States.

Figure 7.5. View south of the east side of Split Mountain Gorge. Gypsum mining is shown at center left. Ridge-capping rock layer is Miocene Split Mountain sturzstrom (catastrophic rock flow).

After reveling in the desert scenery and ambiance, drive up Fish Creek Wash, enter the stratigraphy exposed in Split Mountain Gorge, and proceed to the Wall.

STOP 2: THE WALL
After driving south into Split Mountain Gorge for about 0.5 mile, stop beneath the tall wall of conglomerate (Figure 7.6) on your right

Figure 7.6. The Wall on the west side of Split Mountain Gorge. Two Miocene alluvial fans are exposed on this fault-cut face. Near the base are reddish strata cut off on top by an angular uncon- formity (see arrow), which is overlain by a thick, coarse-grained alluvial fan.

(before the stream takes a big bend to the left). Look for the following:

- Notice the faults cutting the steep cliff face. They are part of the fault system that was later eroded to form Split Mountain Gorge. Match up the rock layers across each fault and deter- mine which side moved up and which moved down. Is there also horizontal offset on the faults? Yes—beds matched across the faults differ in thickness, indicating horizontal offset of beds that vary in thickness.

- Near the base of the cliff are reddish sandstone beds with conglomerates; they are cut by an irregular erosion surface (indicated by the arrow in Figure 7.6). This erosion surface is buried by the thick pile of conglomerate and sandstone beds that make up most of the cliff. The reddish beds below the erosional unconformity are part of a poorly developed, local alluvial fan. The reddish fan developed alongside volcanic flow rock in nearby areas, recording an early phase of extension and rifting from 22 to 14 million years ago. In nearby areas, Charlie Winker reports marine fossils encrusting some of the volcanic rocks, showing that Gulf of California seawater flooded part of this rift basin in mid-Miocene time.

- Above the unconformity is a 0.25-mile thick mass of alluvial-fan strata. Dennis Kerr has subdivided the massive alluvial-fan deposits into subenvironments based on the relative proportions of channel-fill, debris-flow, and sheet-flood strata. The beds making up most of the Wall accumulated high on the Miocene alluvial fan. Notice the abundance of boulder-dominated, debris-flow deposits; these deposits contain some striking examples of reverse grading where large boulders are near the tops of sedimentary beds, indicating that they were carried on top of gravity-pulled debris flows. Most of the sandstone beds were deposited from sheet-like flood waters. The alluvial-fan strata have east-directed sedimentary structures and fabric, eastward fining of grain sizes, and eastward thinning of the entire body of sediment. The evidence all indicates derivation from the Vallecito Mountains. Also, the rock types of the conglomerate-clast population are dominated by plutonic rocks that resemble the bedrock of the eastern Vallecito Mountains.

- Facing up the gorge, look southeast about 0.5 mile to see the light-colored sandstone beds with numerous small caves cut into them. This will be Stop 3.

Return to your vehicle and drive around the big bend in Fish Creek Wash (Figure 7.3); park at the mouth of the tributary stream that rises to the east. Hike up the tributary stream canyon to your left (east) for about 330 yards. Notice that you are moving *down* the sequence of rock layers as you climb *up* the stream canyon. You are going back in time to the deposits left by a major, north-flowing braided stream (Figure 7.7). Your eastward climb up the steep floor of the tributary channel has let you become enveloped in the Amphitheater.

Figure 7.7. Cavernous-weathering sandstones deposited in a north-flowing Miocene braided stream.

STOP 3: THE AMPHITHEATER

Look to the south, to the east, to the north—what an impressive sight. You are enclosed within cavernous-weathering, light-colored, coarse sandstone. The volume of sandstone appears exaggerated because you are standing in the axis of the Split Mountain anticline (Figure 7.7).

Look back to the west and assess the relationship of these sandstone strata with the coarse-grained, eastward-built alluvial fan strata of the Wall. Are the beds around you older (superpositionally lower), younger (higher), or on the same depositional level with the alluvial-fan strata? To answer this question, visualize the 3D and 4D relationships between the alluvial fan of Stop 2 and the braided-stream sandstones of this stop. Braided stream valleys are so choked with sediment that the flowing water is overwhelmed, forcing the water to divide and recombine like a braid. Visualize an elongate, tilted valley occupied by a large braided stream that flows to the north; at the same time, from the Vallecito Mountains on the west side of the valley, a massive alluvial fan is building eastward. The fan eventually overran the braided stream from the side, blocking the stream's course.

The plutonic and metamorphic clasts in the sandstone beds were derived in part from the Fish Creek Mountains. The limited range and number of sedimentary structures help define a braided-stream environment. The low-angle cross beds to the north and the inclined clasts tilted to the south indicate a northerly paleoflow direction. In 1984 Dennis Kerr interpreted the strata as a braided stream that flowed northward along the axis of a drainage basin in a region with considerable topographic relief.

Visualize the Miocene struggle for space where you are now standing. A big braided stream is flowing northward along its fault-created floor while being crowded out by a massive, eastward-growing alluvial fan. On the way back down to your vehicle, walk slowly and inspect the individual sedimentation units. The beds record the battle for space that occurred as debris flows and sheet floods from the lower slope of the alluvial fan intruded into the floodplain of the braided stream. A wealth of sedimentary structures are exposed here: graded beds, reverse grading, hyperconcentrated flows, flame structures, weakly developed paleosols (ancient soils), liquefaction, climbing ripples, boulder trains, and minor channels.

After enjoying the sedimentary structures, return to your vehicle and proceed up the wash about 0.4 mile until you see on your left the massive and steep gray wall of sedimentary rock known as the Face.

STOP 4: THE FACE

The vertical Face is the basal portion of a voluminous, quartz-cemented sturzstrom deposit composed dominantly of shattered plutonic rock from the Vallecito Mountains (Figure 7.8). Sturzstrom events are the most spectacular of all mass movements. The term *sturzstrom* is from the German words *sturz* (fall) and *strom* (stream). Sturzstroms occur when a rock mass with a volume in excess of one million cubic yards falls near vertically, shatters, and flows outward as a dry "fluid" at incredible speeds. A modern sturzstrom event occurred in 1970 in Peru when a 100-million-cubic-yard mass flowed 10 miles at a velocity of up to 210 miles per hour, killing 18,000 people.

Figure 7.8. The Face is a vertical cliff atop the east wall of Split Mountain Gorge. It is the lower part of a deposit left by a high-speed, catastrophic flow (Split Mountain sturzstrom) that raced southeast across the Miocene topography. The middle third of the slope (between the arrows) is the red-and-grey sturzstrom deposit.

The Face is composed of the basal Split Mountain sturzstrom identified by Dennis Kerr and myself (Kerr and Abbott, 1996). The lower portion is exposed here, at Stop 4, and its upper portion will be examined at Stop 5. This sturzstrom mass sits on a slightly older sturzstrom deposit, the red-and-grey sturzstrom (see middle part of Figure 7.8, between the arrows). The red-and-grey sturzstrom lies on top of the alluvial-fan strata viewed at Stops 2 and 3.

The red-and-grey sturzstrom had been interpreted earlier as contorted alluvial-fan strata deformed by the violent passage of the Split Mountain sturzstrom above it. This interpretation is not accurate, however, because (1) the rumpled red-and-grey mass displays sturzstrom fabric such as jigsaw-puzzle texture; (2) sediment-filled stream channels are cut into the red-and-grey mass (Figure 7.9); and (3) the passage of the overlying Split Mountain sturzstrom did not disturb the underlying beds like rumpling a carpet; instead the action was more like a knife passing through butter, creating "decapitated stones" as shown in Figure 7.10.

Figure 7.9. Close-up of contact between red-and-grey sturzstrom mass and overlying Split Mountain sturzstrom deposit. Arrow points to sediment-filled stream channel formed between the two sturzstrom events.

Figure 7.10. Close-up of stream-channel deposit shown in Figure 7.9. Arrow points to boulder sliced in half by the fast-moving Split Mountain sturzstrom, which decapitated the stone and left grooves on top.

The big eastward-building alluvial fan experienced at least two separate events when voluminous masses of Vallecito Mountains bedrock fell, shattered, and then flowed to the east down the Miocene topography to the north-trending axial valley. The eastward flow was documented by Steve Borron, who measured the orientations of grooves scratched in rocks underlying the flowing sturzstrom.

After observing contact relationships and the internal fabric at the Face, the great volume of the Split Mountain sturzstrom compels us to drive another 0.2 mile up the wash to view the top of the sturzstrom at the Boulder Bed.

STOP 5: THE BOULDER BED
Locating Stop 5 is not difficult—the gigantic boulders of plutonic rock on your left (east) are too stunning to drive past (Figure 7.11).

Figure 7.11. View east over the top of the Boulder Bed. These mega-boulders of plutonic rock from the Vallecito Mountains rode on top of the high-velocity Split Mountain sturzstrom. The light-colored band of rock on the eastern skyline is the Fish Creek Gypsum.

This is the top of the Split Mountain sturzstrom mass; it is marked by the mega-boulders that rode on top of the high-velocity sturzstrom. Down inside the flowing sturzstrom the masses of fallen plutonic rock were being fractured into innumerable pieces, while big boulders that began the ride on top stayed whole only by staying up high and on top of the moving mass. Imagine you were here 5.4 million years ago when a great earthquake shook loose a 300-million-cubic-yard mass of plutonic rocks high up the steep face of the Vallecito Mountains. The mass fell rapidly, hit and shattered on impact with the alluvial fan, and then flowed southeast at speeds of 100–200 miles per hour. The speed is estimated from comparable events at Elm, Switzerland, in 1881, and at Jungay, Peru, in 1970.

Take a close look at the following features in the Split Mountain sturzstrom deposit:

- The whole thick mass is dominantly composed of just one type of plutonic rock. On close inspection notice that even the fine-grained material is just shattered remains of this one plutonic rock.
- Impact fracture patterns can be seen in the mega-boulders.
- In some places a jigsaw-puzzle texture can be seen; and pieces of shattered rock, after having flowed for miles, can still be visually restored to their original pre-flow positions. This jigsaw-puzzle texture is most easily seen in shattered pegmatites. (Pegmatites form from white-colored, late-stage magma that crystallizes inside cracks in rocks, producing tabular bodies.) The jigsaw-puzzle texture is mind-boggling.

By what mechanism does a dry bedrock mass shatter and then flow at high velocity without its broken pieces becoming mixed up? A unique deposit requires a unique mechanism of movement. Jay Melosh thinks the incredible speeds achieved are due to trapped acoustic (sound) energy and vibrations within the moving mass that reduce the coefficient of internal friction; he calls this process *acoustic fluidization*. It is a unique mechanism and may explain the sturzstrom phenomenon of high-speed flow of dry materials over long distances. Additional energy may be gained by moving over ground that is shaking dramatically during an earthquake. (The popular idea of high-velocity flow occurring on top of a compressed carpet of air does *not* fit the field data.)

So what happened here? In latest Miocene time, presumably initiated by a great earthquake, a 300-million-cubic-yard mass of pegmatite-cut plutonic rock fell from the Vallecito Mountains, shattered, and raced eastward for over 7 miles down the alluvial fan, up the braided stream valley, and finally slammed into the Fish Creek Mountains. The waters of the Gulf of California entered this area very shortly thereafter.

Did the Split Mountain sturzstrom mass fill part of the braided-stream valley and act as a permeable barrier, isolating an arm of marine water and thus allowing it to evaporate and form the Fish Creek Gypsum body? Marlene Dean has shown that the gypsum is a north-northwest elongated mass about 6 miles long and 3 miles wide, with its greatest thickness (up to 235 feet) occurring in a northwest-southeast trend. The gypsum body has the same trend and shape as the braided stream valley—why the coincidence?

Looking eastward and upward, notice the light-colored rock body capping the skyline ridge to the east (Figure 7.11)—this rock body is the Fish Creek Gypsum and is part of the same rock body you saw from Stop 1 being mined. The gypsum (calcium sulphate) body is up to 235 feet thick and was formed by evaporation of ancient marine water. Marlene Dean found thin clay layers within the gypsum that contain marine microfossils of late Miocene–early Pliocene age. The gypsum sits on top of the Split Mountain sturzstrom deposit, as can be seen on the eastern skyline and by walking up narrow canyons heading east. Here is an intriguing question: did the same giant earthquake that unleashed the Split Mountain sturzstrom event also change the landscape enough to let in the ocean? Gypsum sitting on top of the Split Mountain sturzstrom clearly indicates that the ocean flooded the region shortly after the sturzstrom flowed. Once seawater covered the area, evaporation caused the salts in the seawater to become concentrated, which led to the precipitation of gypsum.

Ponder the following for a while—below the Split Mountain sturzstrom lies a 1-mile thick nonmarine pile of braided-stream and alluvial-fan strata; above the sturzstrom is a 2.6-mile thick marine section of gypsum, shallow shelf, and Colorado River delta strata. Again the question arises—did the same great earthquakes that unleashed the sturzstrom flows also let in water from the Gulf of California?

Standing in Fish Creek Wash and looking to the southeast you will see greenish mudstone with light-colored sandstone beds sitting on top of the Split Mountain sturzstrom deposit (Figure 7.12). These sediments are part of an alluvial fan composed of locally derived sediments that built into the marine water as a delta (fan delta). A short walk eastward up the tributary canyon at the base of the green mudstone beds shows green mudstone sitting on top of sturzstrom boulders. Continuing up the canyon another 100 yards you will find gypsum draped over the top of the sturzstrom boulders (Figure 7.13). Why the change? Can you visualize the landscape here in late Miocene time? Put on your 3D and 4D thinking

Figure 7.12. View southeast of marine fan-delta mudstone and sand-stone deposited on top of the Split Mountain sturzstrom mass. Walk up the side canyon to see the Fish Creek Gypsum overlying the sturzstrom deposit (Figure 7.13).

cap and visualize the sturzstrom deposit being flooded by the ocean and then gypsum crystallizing from the evaporating water; at the same time, a fan delta is forming and building across one segment of the seashore.

In the fan-delta sandstones, notice the following:

- Graded beds that formed when suspended sediment in seawater settled out, coarsest grains first.
- Burrows and tracks of invertebrate organisms.
- Flame structures.
- Ripped-up (eroded) mud clasts.
- Solemarks on the base of sandstone beds where currents eroded the sea-floor mud leaving grooves that were later filled by sand casts.

Returning to Fish Creek Wash, look for evidence of the fault system eroded by Fish Creek to make the Split Mountain Gorge.

Figure 7.13. Gypsum precipitated from seawater on top of boulders capping the Split Mountain sturzstrom deposit. This marks the first entry of seawater into the Miocene Split Mountain Gorge area.

How do we recognize a fault? By the offset of once-continuous rock bodies. Standing in the wash, look to the east side at the green mudstones sitting on the sturzstrom boulders. Now look to the west side—do the rock layers continue from the east side to the west side? You will notice that they do not. Look carefully and match up the rock layers from east side to west side. What is the direction of fault offset? Has the west side moved toward the north (down the wash), or has it moved to the south (up the wash)? You are now involved in solving a real-life geologic problem.

Let's make one more observation before leaving this fascinating location. Look up to the southeastern and southwestern skylines. Do you see the broken-up conglomeratic mass capping the ridges? This mass is another sturzstrom deposit from a younger event that fell from the Fish Creek Mountains and raced through seawater toward the northwest. We will take a close look at these deposits at the head of the gorge at Stop 7.

Return to your vehicle and drive another 0.25 mile farther up the wash through the marine fan-delta strata until you see the crazy folds of the Split Mountain Gorge anticline.

STOP 6: SPLIT MOUNTAIN GORGE ANTICLINE

Notice the dramatic fold in the west wall of the gorge (Figure 7.14). It is an asymmetrical anticline formed by compressing once

Figure 7.14. The Split Mountain Gorge anticline was created when a mass detached from the moving Fish Creek sturzstrom and plowed into the sea floor, crumpling up some fan-delta sand beds.

horizontal sediment layers (the State Park Service has placed a descriptive monument here). The anticline involves sandstone beds of the marine fan delta. Also evident here is the shattered plutonic and metamorphic debris of the subaqueous Fish Creek sturzstrom as well as several faults. What force caused the anticline? The anticline was formed over 5 million years ago when a portion of the fast-moving sturzstrom (rock flow) slammed into the sea floor, causing the water-saturated sand layers to deform.

By crawling up and around the steep slopes here, you can find sand pillars that injected from the fan-delta sands into the sturzstrom mass in flame-structure style; this demonstrates that the two masses mingled while both were still soft sediment. This outcrop has confused a few people because it is cut across by faults; but the faults are millions of years younger and had nothing to do with forming the anticline.

Continue up the wash to the mouth of Crazycline Canyon (Figure 7.3).

STOP 7: THE CRAZYCLINES

The wild anticlinal (upwarp) and synclinal (downwarp) folds have been called crazyclines by Charlie Winker, a name that becomes ever-more apt if you walk up Crazycline Canyon. The crazyclines were created by the deformation of submerged, marine fan-delta beds from the high-velocity passage of a subaqueous sturzstrom. Some of this sturzstrom is represented by the chaotic breccia shown in Figure 7.15.

Around 5.2 million years ago, a 300-million-cubic-yard mass was dislodged from the mixed plutonic/pegmatitic/metamorphic rocks of the Fish Creek Mountains. This event resulted in the Fish Creek sturzstrom that flowed westward across a shallow marine ledge, entered deeper water, and then ran across a prograding fan delta before ending as a more traditional conglomerate nearly 7 miles away from its source. En route, portions of the sturzstrom deformed the underlying sediments; lobes of the sturzstrom both injected and sank into the bottom sediments, causing the fan-delta sediment layers to fold and uprise in deformed masses greater than 115 feet thick.

Inspect the outcrop on the north wall of the canyon (Figure 7.15). What is the nature of the contact between the fan-delta sandstone/ conglomerate and the Fish Creek sturzstrom breccia? How can you tell these conglomerates apart? (Check the roundness of the boulders—boulders in the fan delta were rolled around by marine water and are rounded, whereas the boulders in the sturzstrom were shattered and are angular.) Is the texture of the subaqueous sturzstrom different from that of the subaerial sturzstrom deposits seen at Stops 4 and 5? (Look for jigsaw-puzzle patterns.) Are there differences in the rock types of the conglomerate clasts that allow you to distinguish the Fish Creek sturzstrom from the Split Mountain sturzstrom? (Hint: the Vallecito Mountains are mostly intermediate plutonic rock, whereas the Fish Creek Mountains have significant amounts of whitish granite, dark metamorphic rocks—mica schist, gneiss—and mega-pegmatites.)

Figure 7.15. At the head of Split Mountain Gorge, on the south-facing canyon wall, the chaotic conglomerate (breccia) of the Fish Creek sturzstrom deposit can be seen where it overran marine sandstone beds of the fan delta.

The subaqueous sturzstrom deposit (Fish Creek sturzstrom) has features in common with the subaerial sturzstrom (Split Mountain sturzstrom); for example, both deposits display a jigsaw-puzzle texture, both lack internal mixing within shattered bedrock domains, and both have rocks composed of the same materials (shown through chemical and X-ray diffraction analyses of clasts and nearby matrix). These shared characteristics show that the mechanism of movement for sturzstroms is the same whether travel is subaerial or subaqueous.

Let's move up wash, out of the gorge for a short distance, and search for the arrival of the Colorado River delta.

STOP 8: COLORADO RIVER DELTA

How can you recognize when the Colorado River began dumping its voluminous load of sediments into this area? To get started, walk or drive about 200 yards up creek from the head of the gorge and look for the outcrop shown in Figure 7.16. All of the sedimentary rocks examined on the trip so far have been derived locally by erosion and transportation from nearby mountains. But local sediments changed to regionally derived sediments abruptly. Charlie Winker showed the position in the sedimentary sequence where the Colorado River first began dumping its tremendous volumes of sediment—the position is indicated by the arrow in Figure 7.16. Once the Colorado River began dumping its sediments here about 5.2 million years ago, the entire character of the region changed. We have seen the record of earlier events: local north-flowing braided stream overrun by east-building alluvial fan from the Vallecito Mountains, then catastrophic sturzstrom events, flooding by the ocean with gypsum precipitating from the evaporating seawater at the same time a fan delta built across the shoreline only to be overrun by another sturzstrom; all of this local complexity was overwhelmed by the voluminous Colorado River and its massive load of sediment. If you drive farther up Fish Creek you will climb through sediments thousands of feet thick that were deposited by the Colorado River and that blanketed the Salton Trough during much of Pliocene time.

Consider the tectonic setting. How could the Colorado River delta have been here? The plate-tectonic history of this region tells us that 5.5 million years ago, what we now know as the Gulf of California was just beginning to open as a consequence of sea-floor spreading. Where would the Split Mountain region have been then? The answer is, to the south, in the modern-day state of Sonora, Mexico. Visualize sea-floor spreading tearing the Californias off mainland Mexico and moving the peninsula 2.2 inches (5.6 cm) per year toward the northwest. What path would the Split Mountain region follow? From way down south it moved slowly to the northwest, riding on the Pacific plate. By 4 million years ago, the Split Mountain region had drifted in front of the Colorado River mouth, which sat then, as now, on the North American plate. When the Colorado River delta began depositing its voluminous load of sediments in this area, it overwhelmed and buried most of the varied and complex local features we have been examining. And then, as the area continued drifting to the northwest, it left the Colorado River delta behind.

Figure 7.16. The sandstone beds shown in the upper part of the photo (beginning at the arrow) were deposited by the Colorado River when it first arrived in this region.

How can you recognize Colorado River sands from locally derived sands? Gordon Gastil used a hand-held magnetic-susceptibility meter to measure the amount of magnetite in the sandstone. How does this device help us here? The plutonic rocks of the eastern Peninsular Ranges contain very little magnetite, and the sediments derived from them yield a weak magnetic susceptibility signature. All the rocks you've seen in this field trip—braided stream, alluvial fan, fan delta, and sturzstroms—contain negligible amounts of magnetite and therefore have low magnetic susceptibility. However, the sediments that have been eroded from 13 western states by the Colorado River contain appreciable magnetite. Thus we can locate the arrival of Colorado River sands at the first sandstone bed with high magnetic susceptibility readings. The high readings continue upward through a thick sequence of sandstones.

Continental Borderland

During late Oligocene and Miocene time, an unusual topography formed offshore in the Southern California–Baja California continental borderland (Figure 7.17). The edge of the North American continent was tectonically extended and faulted, forming a topography of ridges and basins. Eric Frost visualizes this crustal extension as an effect of the breaking-up at depth of the subducting Farallon oceanic plate (Figure 6.1). As the subducting oceanic plate disintegrated, the overlying brittle continental crust was extended and pulled apart along numerous faults (Figure 7.18). The continental borderland topography was similar to that formed by extensional processes in the Salton Trough on the east side of the Peninsular Ranges and throughout much of the western United States in Miocene time. Eric Frost explains that extension occurred on both sides of and beneath the Peninsular Ranges that lay as a "strong coherent beam" on top of the extending crust below. The extension that dominated Miocene time was replaced in dominance during Pliocene time by the horizontal-displacement faulting that continues today.

Along coastal southern California and northern Baja California, some of the extended land was raised above sea level while other areas sank to form deep basins (Figure 7.17). Uplifted high-

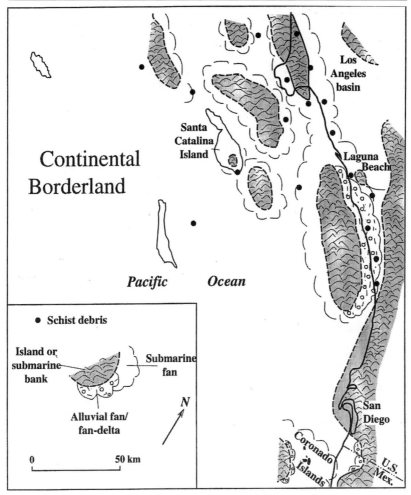

Figure 7.17. Schematic map of Miocene highlands squeezed up on land and above sea level and the alluvial fans shed from them. After Stuart, 1979.

lands of igneous and metamorphic rocks were eroded and shed sedimentary debris into adjoining basins as alluvial fans and fan deltas. Miocene events were different—much of the sediment transport

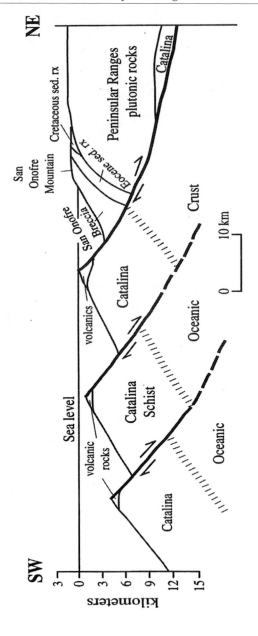

Figure 7.18. Cross section from San Onofre Mountain (near I-5 immigration checkpoint) to offshore. Notice the faults and how the area has been pulled apart. Erosion of the Catalina Schist provided most of the debris for the San Onofre Breccia.

was from topographic highs in the west, with sediment transport to the east! Think about this topography—it represents a major departure from the usual order of business where highlands stand in the east and sediment transport is to the west.

Where can we see the rocks involved in Miocene events? Good outcrops of basement rock that stood as highlands are exposed at Santa Catalina Island and in part of the Palos Verdes Hills in Los Angeles. Conglomeratic sedimentary masses eroded from local highlands are exposed in the beach cliffs of Laguna Beach and at Dana Point in Orange County, in the San Onofre Mountains in Camp Pendleton, in northern Oceanside, at the southern three Coronado Islands, and south of Tijuana near La Joya. Although there are numerous outcrops, most of them are difficult to visit. Our best bets are (1) to drive to the beach cliffs at Dana Point in Orange County, (2) to obtain permission from the U.S. Marine Corps to inspect the west-facing slope of the San Onofre Mountains along the east side of Interstate 5 in Camp Pendleton, or (3) to visit outcrops in northern Oceanside.

Miocene Field Trip: Rock Collecting in Northern Oceanside

Superb Miocene conglomerate outcrops have been cut and shaped along the southeastern side of Highway 76 just east of Interstate 5. Unfortunately these bluish-gray conglomerate outcrops are sealed off by freeway fences, and parking is illegal. For a close-up look at the Miocene conglomerate-clast suite, exit Interstate 5 at Oceanside Boulevard and travel west for 0.43 mile (Figure 7.19; and *Thomas Guide,* p. 1106, C2). As you drive uphill, the roadcuts on your right expose the Miocene San Onofre Breccia (a breccia is a conglomerate with angular clasts). At the top of the hill, turn right on Nevada Street and immediately park. Now walk back downhill and look at the outcrop. It is easy to collect the conglomerate clasts that have washed onto the sidewalk.

What kinds of strange rocks exist here that led to the unusual tectonic hypotheses invoked to explain them? The rocks here are unusual and unlike any other rocks we see in San Diego. During Miocene time in San Diego there were hills and mountains to the west and sediment was washed east to the continent. This is an unusual topography and it involves unusual rocks.

We can best read the Miocene history here by examining the San Onofre Breccia clasts eroded from the fault-uplifted highlands and deposited in the adjoining lowlands (Figure 7.17). The formation name is taken from Mount San Onofre, which lies just east of the immigration checkpoint on Interstate 5 in Camp Pendleton. The San Onofre Breccia is mostly 17–14 million years old and is composed of clasts from a variety of source rocks.

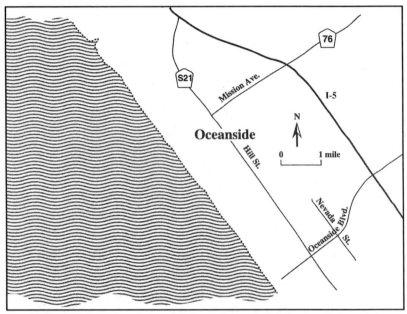

Figure 7.19. Location map for Miocene field trip, Oceanside.

The rock types have been well described by A. O. Woodford and later by Charlie Stuart (Stuart, 1979). Bring a rock identification book with you, for these rocks are challenging to identify. They include (1) blueschist with a distinctive blue-gray color imparted by the mineral glaucophane; (2) greenschist with a greenish color imparted by the minerals epidote, chlorite, and actinolite; (3) quartz schist, (4) saussuritized gabbro containing actinolite as an alteration product; (5) amphibolite with coarsely crystalline, blackish amphibole plus other minerals such as zoisite, garnet, and albite feldspar; (6) serpentinite; (7) vein rocks of quartz; (8) clasts from nearly contemporaneous volcanic rocks; (9) reworked Poway rhyolite clasts; and (10) some ripped-up and redeposited hunks of sedimentary rock. Rock types 1–7 are all derived from a rock body known as the Catalina Schist (Figure 7.18), which takes its name from Santa Catalina Island. These metamorphic-rock clasts are unique in San Diego County; they formed under conditions of high pressure and relatively low temperature. The high pressures were due to tectonic-plate compression as the Farallon oceanic plate ran into and beneath the North American plate; temperatures were low because the events occurred near the surface.

The Miocene tectonic regime is in direct contrast to the high-temperature and low-pressure metamorphic rocks altered above the intrusive Cretaceous magma that formed the heart of the Peninsular Ranges. These high-temperature metamorphic rocks take their name from the common exposures around the town of Julian, and they are called Julian Schist.

The San Onofre Breccia clasts offer an excellent range of rocks to examine. Notice the following features:

- The bluish-gray color where the San Onofre Breccia is fresh and unweathered.
- Many clasts within the breccia have tabular shapes with angular edges.
- Ancient channels were broad rather than deep and had low-sloping walls.
- Sedimentary rock layers are marked by different sizes of gravels; for example, beds are dominated by well-sorted small pebbles or poorly sorted cobbles.

How many of the San Onofre Breccia rock types can you find in the Oceanside clast suite? This site affords a good opportunity to extend the range of rocks in your collection. Couple this Oceanside rock-collecting trip with one to the Julian area and you will have collected a wide range of metamorphic rock types.

CHAPTER 8
PLIOCENE HISTORY

The Pliocene is a subdivision of Tertiary time. In 1833, Charles Lyell described the "Newer Pliocene" fossil assemblage as having about 90% of its species still alive today. He recommended the strata at Val di Noto in Sicily as being typical. Today we define Pliocene time as having occurred from 5.3 to 1.8 million years ago. However, there is an unresolved debate about when Pliocene time ends. Many geologists think the boundary should be placed at 2.67 million years ago. This debate will be examined in Chapter 9.

In San Diego, Pliocene rocks are exposed in several areas (see maps in Kennedy and Peterson, 1975; and Kennedy and Tan, 1977). The Pliocene fossil record in San Diego is superb—it contains abundant invertebrates and world-class assemblages of marine mammals, fish, and birds.

Tectonics

Throughout Miocene time, the young oceanic crust subducting beneath western North America supplied heat that aided the tectonic extension of the region. At about 5.5 million years ago, the boundary between the Pacific and North American plates moved eastward to its present-day position in the Gulf of California. The resultant extension and stretching of North American continental crust proceeded so far that asthenosphere rock rose, melted, and initiated the sea-floor spreading (Figure 1.1) that formed, and continues to form, the Gulf of California. Just prior to the beginning of Pliocene time, sea-floor spreading began tearing Baja California and the portion of California west of the San Andreas fault away from the North American plate; the separated continental rock mass continues to move north-northwest, riding on the Pacific plate (Figure 8.1).

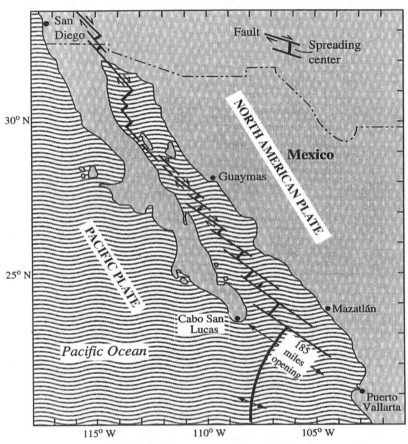

Figure 8.1. Sea-floor spreading began opening the Gulf of Califor-
nia about 5.5 million years ago, just before Pliocene time began.
Since then, Baja California and San Diego have moved about
185 miles to the north-northwest.

The dominant tectonic process affecting San Diego in Pliocene time was the opening of the Gulf of California and the resultant northward movement of the west side of numerous faults, such as the San Andreas, San Jacinto, Elsinore, Rose Canyon, Islas de los Coronados, and San Clemente Island (Figure 8.2). Northward movement of the Pacific plate has carried Baja California, San Diego, Los Angeles, and Santa Cruz some 185 miles in the last 5.5 million years. The tectonic style that began in Pliocene time continues today.

What is happening today along the Pacific–North American plate boundary, that is, the San Andreas fault zone? Baja California and western California are moving north at a rate of about 2.2 inches (5.6 cm) per year. The opening and spreading of the Gulf of California is the driving force behind most California earthquakes. Will San Diego continue to have large earthquakes? Yes. Will California break off during a giant earthquake and sink beneath the ocean waters? No. Is this possible? No. The Californias west of the Gulf of California and the San Andreas fault "broke off" 5.5 million years ago, have not sunk, and cannot sink because continental rock has a lower specific gravity than the rocks beneath it—in other words, the continents float on the denser rocks below.

Pliocene Climate

The global climate has been cooling since the thermal maximum 55 million years ago. Massive glaciers began building on Antarctica by 33 million years ago, but ice sheets in the Northern Hemisphere were not generated and maintained until just 2.67 million years ago. What happened to finally allow major ice sheets to build up in the Northern Hemisphere? The formation of the Isthmus of Panama as an unbroken landmass between North and South America triggered the global climatic cooling that led to the Ice Age. When a continuous land bridge formed between North and South America, it blocked latitudinal circulation of water in the equatorial seas. Trade winds blowing warm equatorial waters to the west piled up in the Caribbean Sea and Gulf of Mexico and were deflected northward, causing the Florida Current and the Gulf Stream that run along the eastern side of North America. When this warm ocean water reached northern polar latitudes, it evaporated in great vol-

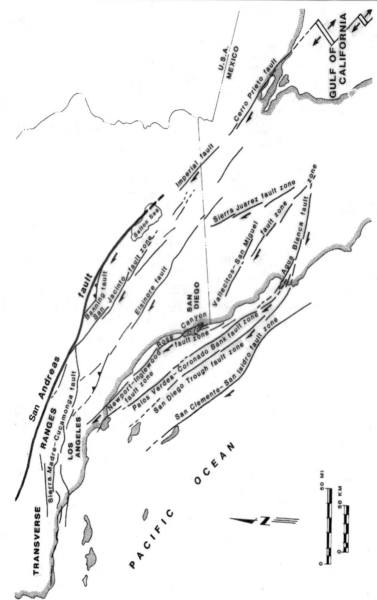

Figure 8.2. Continuing opening of the Gulf of California causes numerous active faults to slice across the Californias.

umes (because warm water evaporates more easily than cold water), falling as snow on northern lands and eventually becoming compacted into continent-burying ice sheets.

CHANGING SEA LEVELS

How was San Diego affected by the late Pliocene buildup of continental glaciers in the Northern Hemisphere? Sea level fell markedly—about 625 feet. The greatest sea-level drops occurred in latest Miocene and earliest Pliocene time (5.5–5.0 million years ago); the greatest global sea-level drop was about 800 feet. Sea level was so low in the Atlantic Ocean that no water flowed into the Mediterranean Sea. It took only about 1,000 years of Mediterranean sunshine to evaporate the Mediterranean Sea and convert it to a dry canyon that bottomed out at 10,000 feet below sea level. What a canyon! The total drying of the Mediterranean Sea was repeated numerous times.

How stable are the continental ice sheets, and how are sea levels affected when they melt? Continental ice sheets are not very stable; they have advanced and retreated in cycles lasting about 100,000 years. On time scales measured in thousands of years, sea levels have risen and fallen about 600 feet as a result of glaciers melting or forming. Today we are most of the way into an interglacial interval. The ice sheets burying Canada, Scandinavia, and Siberia just 20,000 years ago have melted, causing global sea level to rise 425 feet. But Antarctica and Greenland are still buried beneath ice. What would happen to sea level if these ice sheets were to melt? Global sea level would rise about 210 feet.

Visualize the San Diego shoreline of today, and then picture it with a sea level that is 210 feet higher. What you are picturing occurred in San Diego numerous times in the last 2.67 million years. Figure 8.3 shows a typical San Diego shoreline in Pliocene time. At times of high sea level, San Diego was submerged beneath a broad, ocean-filled embayment akin to a miniature Monterey Bay. The Pliocene San Diego embayment provided various subenvironments for organisms to inhabit such as sea cliff, rocky and sandy beaches, river delta, and nearshore submarine shelf. Sands and gravels washed into the broad bay. The waters of the bay were home to clams, snails, sea urchins, and other invertebrates. Fish teemed in the bay water to the delight of a large population of birds. The bay attracted fur seals, walruses, whales, and other marine mammals. This oceanic zoo of Pliocene animals is preserved as fossils in the San Diego Formation throughout the metropolitan region of San Diego, National City, and Chula Vista.

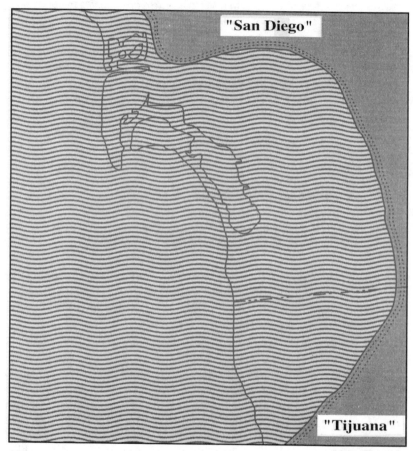

Figure 8.3. The shoreline of the San Diego region in late Pliocene time looked like a miniature Monterey Bay.

Pliocene Formation

Pliocene rocks in San Diego were discussed first in 1874 as part of W. H. Dall's description of molluscan fossils. In 1898, Dall called these rock layers the "San Diego beds;" today these layers are referred to as the San Diego Formation. Dall's 19th-century descriptions came from two primary localities: (1) a well in Balboa Park that has long since been filled in as part of the Cabrillo Freeway (Highway 163) right-of-way, and (2) the strata in the sea cliffs in Pacific Beach and on the southern side of Mount Soledad. We will visit the Pacific Beach outcrops on the Tourmaline Surfing Park field trip. (For more information on the Pliocene of San Diego, see Hertlein and Grant, 1944; and Deméré, 1983.)

The San Diego Formation is as much as 280 feet thick. In general, its lower subdivision is thicker, is dominated by fine sand, and was deposited in shallow seawater. The upper subdivision is thinner, has coarser grain sizes with conglomerates common, and much of the sediment accumulated in nonmarine environments. Trends within the San Diego Formation are coarsening-upward grain sizes and shallowing-upward water depths.

The abundant mollusc and microfossil data indicate that the San Diego Formation accumulated in late Pliocene time and crossed the boundary into early Pleistocene time. The rocks and fossils range in age from about 3 to 1.5 million years old. The fossils also tell something about the water temperatures when the organisms were alive. The organisms found as fossils in the lower San Diego Formation lived in warmer water, about 68°F, and those found as fossils in the upper San Diego Formation lived in cooler water, about 59°F. The cooling of seawater during San Diego Formation time is part of the global temperature decline accompanying our entry into the current Ice Age.

Pliocene Fossils

The San Diego Formation is world renown for its rich assemblages of marine invertebrates and vertebrates. The formation also contains less abundant fossils of terrestrial plants such as pine, oak, cottonwood, avocado, and laurel, and land vertebrates such as giant camel, horse, deer, wolf, peccary, skunk, and gomphothere, an elephant cousin.

MARINE INVERTEBRATES

The fossil molluscs have been the object of enough scientific attention to define more than 140 species of pelecypods (clams, oysters, scallops) and 106 species of gastropods (snails). Investigators include Ulysses S. Grant IV, the grandson of the Civil War commanding general and 18th president of the United States. U. S. Grant IV is senior author of a 1,036-page volume on the Pliocene and Pleistocene marine molluscs of California. Other invertebrate phyla described include the Echinodermata, with seven species of sea urchins, four species of sand dollars, and one species of sea star; Arthropoda, with nine species of barnacles and three species of crab; Brachiopoda, with four species of lamp shells; and Coelenterates, with six species of solitary coral.

Analysis of individual rock layers can tell us about their depositional environment. For example, sandstone beds containing abundant shells of the sand dollar *Dendraster ashleyi,* the surf clam *Tivela stultorum*, and the clam *Spisula catilliformis* indicate that sediments were deposited in shallow marine water just offshore from a sandy beach. Sandstone beds containing abundant shells of the large scallop *Patinopecten healeyi,* the turret snail *Turritella cooperi,* and the clams *Lucinoma annulata* and *Miltha xantusi* tell us that sediments accumulated on the continental shelf.

FISHES

The San Diego Formation also has yielded a large and diverse assemblage of late Pliocene fish (Gottfried, 1982). The fossil assemblage contains over 17 species of sharks and rays, including great white shark (*Carcharodon carcarius*), bay shark (*Carcharhinus sp.*), thresher shark (*Alopias sp.*), hammerhead shark (*Sphyrna sp.*), seven-gill shark (*Hexanchus sp.*), salmon shark (*Lamna sp.*), angel shark (*Squatina sp.*), mako shark (*Isurus sp.*), basking shark (*Cetorhinus sp.*), skates (*Raja spp.*), manta ray (*Morbula sp.*), and bat ray (*Myliobatis sp.*) (Figure 8.4). Because sharks' cartilaginous skeletons usually do not fossilize, only shark teeth are generally preserved in the fossil record, and this is the case in the San Diego Formation. A paleontological dig in Mission Hills excavated an area of about 20 square yards and recovered over 200 individual shark teeth, including several 3-inch-long great white shark teeth. Assuming a ratio of 7 feet of body length to 1 inch of tooth length, we can estimate that the shark would have been 21 feet long.

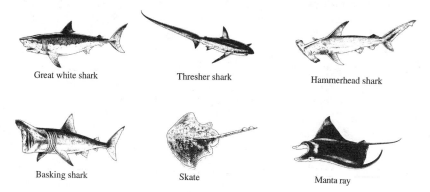

Great white shark   Thresher shark   Hammerhead shark

Basking shark   Skate   Manta ray

Figure 8.4. Modern representatives of some late Pliocene fossil fish in the San Diego Formation.

The San Diego Formation contains fossils of over 50 species of bony fish, including halibut, sheephead, tuna, croaker, sardine, bill fish, surf perch, herring, turbot, queen fish, sand dab, eel, lantern fish, porcupine fish, and sea bass. Skeletal remains of bony fish generally include isolated vertebrae and, rarely, skull and dental material. However, the majority of fish are known only from otoliths, small bony "ear" ossicles that function in maintaining equilibrium.

BIRDS
The assemblage of fossil birds from the San Diego Formation is the most diverse known in the world from Pliocene marine rocks. So far, 24 species of Pliocene marine bird fossils have been found, including grebe (*Podiceps spp.*), albatross (*Diomedea howardae*), shearwater (*Puffinus gilmorei*), gannet and boobie (*Morus recentior* and *Sula clarki*), cormorant (*Phalacrocorax kennelli*), surf scooter (*Mel-*

anitta ceruttii), plover (*Charadrius sp.*), tern (*Sterna sp.*), auklet (*Brachyramphus pliocenum*), murrelet (*Synthliboramphus rineyi*), and flightless auk (*Mancalla spp.*)(Figure 8.5). The extinct flightless auks are represented by at least three species: *M. diegensis, M. milleri,* and *M. emlongi*). Species of flightless auks in the Northern Hemisphere probably occupied the ecological niche filled in the Southern Hemisphere by penguins; both groups of birds are flightless and are generally differentiated by body size. Skeletal remains of flightless auk are quite common at some collecting sites in the San Diego Formation, suggesting that they, like modern penguins, lived in large social flocks. Bird fossils from the San Diego Formation most commonly consist of isolated wing and leg bones. Less common are the delicate bones of the sternum and skull.

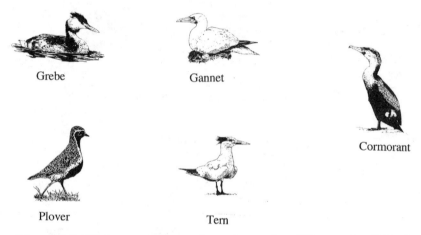

Grebe

Gannet

Cormorant

Plover

Tern

Figure 8.5. Modern representatives of some late Pliocene fossil birds in the San Diego Formation.

MARINE MAMMALS
The marine mammal assemblage from the San Diego Formation is diverse. To date it has yielded three species of pinnipeds: fur seal (*Callorhinus gilmorei*), tuskless walrus (*Dusignathus seftoni*), and tusked walrus (*Valenictus chulavistensis*); seven species of toothed whales including sperm whale (*Scaldicetus sp.*), "river" dolphin

(*Parapontoporia sternbergi*), beluga (*Denebola sp.*), porpoise (*Piscolithax sp.*), and dolphin (*Stenella sp.*); nine species of baleen whales, including various fin whales (*Balaenoptera spp.*); and one sirenian species (*Hydrodamalis cuestae*)(Figure 8.6).

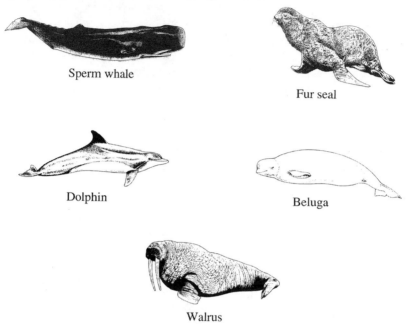

Sperm whale

Fur seal

Dolphin

Beluga

Walrus

Figure 8.6. Modern representatives of some late Pliocene fossil marine mammals in the San Diego Formation.

The presence of walrus and beluga in Pliocene San Diego seems at first to suggest arctic conditions; however, these fossil species and their Miocene ancestors actually evolved in temperate latitudes. The restriction of walrus and beluga to the arctic region did not occur until later in Pleistocene time. Their arctic habitat of today probably indicates a retreat into an arctic refuge.

Walrus

Ecologically, the fossil walrus *Valenictus chulavistaensis* probably lived much like the modern walrus *Odobenus rosmarus*: a shallow-diving, suction feeder that concentrates on benthic marine invertebrate organisms like annelid worms, tunicates, and thin-shelled clams. Skeletal details of the fossil walrus clearly show a close evolutionary relationship or kinship with the modern walrus. In contrast to this similarity with the living species, *Valenictus* had no teeth in its lower jaws and only had enlarged canine teeth (tusks) in its upper jaws. Since the common ancestor of both species possessed teeth, the loss of teeth in *Valenictus* is thought to be an advanced feature. Although the living walrus retains teeth, behavioral studies show that the teeth are not used in feeding. Instead, the animals rely on the strong oral suction produced by their piston-like tongues and strongly vaulted palates; they literally suck thin-shelled and/or soft-bodied animals into their mouths. It is interesting that the dentally more advanced fossil walrus is extinct, whereas the more primitive *Odobenus* is still living.

Whales

The fossil whales from the San Diego Formation differ significantly in size (Deméré, 1981). The baleen whale, *Herpetocetus sp.*, had a skull only 31 inches long with a total body length of less than 13 feet. Compare this relatively small whale with a fossil fin whale, *Balaenoptera sp.*, whose skull measures over 10 feet long and had a total body length estimated at 50 feet.

Pliocene Field Trips

Pliocene strata have been described on two prior field trips; for a more complete understanding of Pliocene time in this region, see the Oligocene field trip along Otay Valley Road in Chapter 6 and the Miocene field trip through Split Mountain Gorge in Chapter 7.

Pliocene Field Trip:
Tourmaline Surfing Park

Tourmaline Surfing Park in Pacific Beach is not just for surfers. The spacious, free parking lot at the foot of Tourmaline Street provides easy access to beautiful beach cliffs (Figure 8.7; and *Thomas Guide,* p. 1247, G5). The sea cliffs expose rocks and fossils from four different times—Cretaceous, Eocene, Pliocene, and Pleistocene. After walking down onto the beach, look far to your right (north) and see the south-facing beach cliff of False Point. The conglomerates in the lower two-thirds of the cliffs are Cretaceous Cabrillo Formation; these rocks were deposited as gravels in the inner-fan valley of a submarine fan. These Cretaceous outcrops sit above (are younger than) the mudstone and sandstone beds viewed during the Cretaceous field trip to La Jolla Bay and La Jolla Cove (see Chapter 3). The Cretaceous submarine fan built westward into the ocean, with coarser grain sizes reaching progressively farther westward with time. The cliffs before you at False Point expose the top of the pile of Cretaceous sedimentary rock layers that began at the south end of La Jolla Shores beach. The False Point rocks were deposited in the ocean 72 million years ago.

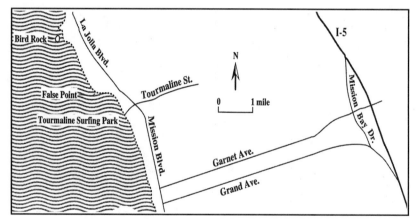

Figure 8.7. Map for Tourmaline Surfing Park field trip.

The west-facing beach cliffs north of the parking lot expose Eocene marine strata. These sedimentary rock layers dip about 11 degrees to the south and display many low-angle planar scour surfaces (Figure 8.8). The Eocene strata are cut off on top by a low-angle planar unconformity on which lies the Pliocene San Diego Formation (Figure 8.9). This unconformity marks a tremendous loss of geologic and paleontologic information. The underlying Eocene

Figure 8.8. Eocene marine strata in sea cliffs north of Tourmaline Street parking lot in Pacific Beach.

Figure 8.9. Sea cliff north of Tourmaline Street parking lot. South-dipping Eocene and Pliocene strata are separated by a planar unconformity representing 43 million years of time.

rocks are about 46 million years old and the overlying Pliocene rocks are less than 3 million years old, thus the unconformity marks the loss of 43 million years of Earth history at this site. What stories of former lives and past events have been lost?

Take a careful look at the unconformity between the Eocene and Pliocene rocks (Figure 8.10). Stand back and notice the following:

Figure 8.10. Contact between Eocene and Pliocene strata on cliffs north of Tourmaline Street parking lot. Sunbather at far right of photo is resting on the unconformity.

- Is the dip (inclination) of the unconformity the same as the dip of the Eocene rock layers? No. The Eocene strata are cut across at a slight angle.
- On top of the unconformity lies the basal conglomerate of the San Diego Formation. Does the conglomerate totally blanket the erosion surface? No. Viewing up-dip to the north, the conglomerate pinches out. This suggests southward-tilting was occurring during deposition of the San Diego Formation. What

caused the tilting? We may be seeing some of the earliest deformation caused by the Rose Canyon fault zone more than 2 million years ago.

Now walk up to the Pliocene basal conglomerate lying on top of the unconformity and examine it carefully. Observe the following:

- Exposure of the erosion surface oxidized the underlying Eocene rocks, turning them red. Look carefully to find small cylindrical holes bored through the hardened erosion surface in the Eocene rocks; these holes were made by rock-boring marine organisms before the Pliocene conglomerate was deposited.
- Examine the rock types of the Pliocene conglomerate clasts (Figure 8.11). What types of rocks do you see? You will see reddish-purplish Poway rhyolite eroded from the Eocene Poway

Figure 8.11. Pliocene conglomerate lying on the Eocene–Pliocene unconformity. Look carefully to see the different clast populations (rounded versus angular) in the conglomerate.

Conglomerate, greenish volcanic breccia from the early Cretaceous Santiago Peak Volcanics, plutonic clasts that commonly
are crumbling due to severe weathering, and some metamorphic rocks such as quartzite.

- Observe the rounding of the Pliocene conglomerate clasts. The
longer a clast is rolled by stream or wave, the smoother and
rounder it becomes. Many clasts are nicely rounded, but others
are angular and appear shattered in place. The angular and
broken clasts probably obtained their shapes at this site as a
result of salt weathering. As salt crystals grow in tiny cracks
they act as levers prying apart and breaking up the host rocks.
(For a discussion of salt weathering, see Peterson, 1979.)

Now move back from the cliff and view the entire Pliocene outcrop in the sea cliff just north of the parking lot (Figure 8.12). The
base of the sea cliff exposes orangish Eocene strata, and the cliff is
topped by dirt-brown-colored Pleistocene sedimentary rocks. Look
at the middle two-thirds of the cliff—the San Diego Formation—
and notice the following:

- Do the Eocene, Pliocene, and Pleistocene strata dip at the same
angle? No—the Eocene rock layers dip the most, the Pliocene
rocks dip less, and the Pleistocene beds dip the least. What do
the varying dips tell us? They indicate that the area has been
subjected to long-term, continuing deformation; the older the
rocks, the more they have been deformed. The varying dip an-
gles probably record the ongoing deformation produced by the
active Rose Canyon fault system, and the movements continue
today.
- Note the geometry of the Pliocene rock layers. Are they lens-
shaped masses filling channels or are they planar-based tabular bodies? Each bed is a planar-based tabular mass that varies
little in its thickness.
- Where do tabular beds of sediment with planar bases accumulate? Mostly in the planar areas just landward or just seaward
of the zone of breaking waves. The basal conglomerate with its
salt-fractured clasts was deposited landward; the overlying beds
with their marine fossils and flat "skipping-stone" clasts formed

seaward. The Pliocene outcrop shown in Figure 8.12 records an initial flooding followed by a slight deepening of seawater.

As you walk south along the beach toward Crystal Pier notice the south-dipping San Diego Formation exposed in the low beach cliffs. Pliocene fossils are common in these rock layers. There are 24 species of scallops listed from the San Diego Formation, includ-

Figure 8.12. Sea cliff just north of Tourmaline Street parking lot. The middle two-thirds of the outcrop is fossiliferous San Diego Formation. Lower quarter of photo shows Eocene strata, upper sixth shows Pleistocene strata.

ing the large, thin-shelled species *Patinopecten healeyi*, which occurs by the thousands in the fossiliferous beds just south of the Tourmaline Street parking lot. Similarly, a shell bed discovered in east San Diego near Interstate 15 and Market Street preserves thousands of disc-shaped external skeletons of the sand dollar *Dendraster ashleyi* in a closely packed concentration with all skeletal "discs" lying horizontal and parallel to bedding.

Walk up to the beach cliffs just south of the Tourmaline Street parking lot. Observe the sandstone and fossils carefully (Figure 8.13).

Figure 8.13. Sea cliff just south of Tourmaline Street parking lot exposes San Diego Formation and profuse concentrations of the large scallop Patinopecten healeyi.

- Notice the layers of fine sandstone (5–6 feet thick), so loose they are burrowed by bees to make homes. The loose and friable nature of the sandstone indicates its geologic youth. It has not been around long enough to be compacted and cemented into a hard rock.

- Notice the scour surfaces in the sandstone. In some places there are concentrations of shells and even hard-rock pebbles lying on the scour surface. These scour surfaces with an overlying load of well-sorted fine sand plus abundant fossils probably were deposited out beyond the breaker zone by a rip current from a major storm or tsunami.

- You cannot help but notice the thousands of thin shells of the Pliocene large scallop *Patinopecten healeyi*. With careful inspection you can also find the cream-colored shells of the large wenteltrap snail *Opalia varicostata*. Other sandstone layers contain different types of scallops, including the finely sculptured *Flabellipecten sternsii* and the small *Argopecten invalidus* and *Argopecten subdolus*. Moving south along the beach, and up through time in the San Diego Formation, you can find another species of scallop, *Pecten bellus,* as well as shells of the Pliocene oyster *Ostrea vespertina* and external skeletons of the sand dollar *Dendraster ashleyi*.

Pliocene Field Trip: South Bay Amphitheater

Pliocene rocks are abundant in southern San Diego. At the southern tip of Paradise Hills, just east of Interstate 805 and north of the South Bay Freeway (54) lies an interesting canyon system herein called the South Bay Amphitheater (Figure 8.14; and *Thomas Guide,* p. 1310, D2). In the canyon at the north end of Calle Abajo, walk into the baseball field area, and you will be surrounded by Pliocene San Diego Formation outcrops. What beautiful exposures of the San Diego Formation! Walk about 60 yards northward along the concrete path on the west side of the baseball fields, past the two-story building, and then notice the following:

- Look over to the east wall of the canyon and let your eyes follow the sedimentary rock layers within the orangish-white San Diego Formation. Individual beds can be traced visually from south to north along the entire east wall. The same beds occur on the northern end of the west wall of the canyon. What happens to the San Diego Formation beds on the west wall as you follow them south toward the building, toward where you are stand-

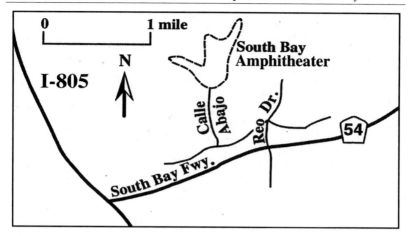

Figure 8.14. Map for South Bay Amphitheater field trip.

ing? The San Diego Formation beds run into dirt-brown Pleistocene sedimentary rocks (Figure 8.15). Why are the dirt-brown Pleistocene rocks on the south sitting side-by-side with the orangish-white Pliocene rocks on the north? This is because one of the La Nacion faults has offset and juxtaposed the two rock masses. Trace the fault surface up the canyon wall. Have the dirt-brown Pleistocene rocks moved up or down relative to the San Diego Formation? They have moved down. Use the law of superposition (described in Chapter 1) to explain why this is so.

• Turn around and look to the southeastern canyon wall, above center field in the lower baseball field. Do you see the uptilted beds of San Diego Formation that bend upward to the south? Why do those rock layers tilt? They are deforming along one of the La Nacion faults. Is the fault still active? Probably. Are baseball fields good things to build on top of an active fault? Yes. If the fault moves two feet, what harm would befall the baseball players?

Walk eastward to the visitors' dugout behind first base on the upper baseball field, and take a look at the beds of the San Diego Formation exposed here (Figure 8.16).

Figure 8.15. View of the west wall of the canyon from the upper base-ball field in the South Bay Amphitheater. Lighter-colored Pliocene San Diego Formation on the north (right) is separated by a fault from darker-colored Pleistocene beds on the south (left).

- Notice the slight downtilt to the north of the San Diego Formation rock layers. Why do they tilt? They are deformed from the horizontal by movements on La Nacion faults.
- Notice the lowermost sedimentary rock layer, the rust-red pebbly sandstone. Is this a marine or nonmarine bed? The bed is nonmarine; the red color comes from oxidation of the Pliocene ground surface, and the angularity of the pebbles shows that they have not been worked and smoothed by ocean waters.
- Notice the whitish coarse sandstone at about knee-to-head height. Examine the sand grain population. What are the sand-grain sizes? Many grains are very coarse. What is the sorting of the sand grains? Poor; there is quite a range of grain sizes. What is the roundness of the larger grains? Angular. Notice the mudstone clasts of up to 2 feet in diameter that were eroded, picked

Figure 8.16. View to the east of San Diego Formation beds behind the first-base dugout at the upper baseball field in the South Bay Amphitheater.

up, and incorporated into this sandstone. Now put these observations together and interpret the rock layer. Is it marine or nonmarine? Large, angular, poorly sorted sand grains with mudstone rip-up clasts tell of a short distance of travel, local erosion by high energy flow, and rapid deposition in a nonmarine environment.

- Notice the 2-foot-thick conglomerate bed about 15 feet up the cliff. What is its geometry? It is a planar-based tabular mass. Examine the conglomerate clasts, many of which are recycled Poway rhyolite clasts. The clasts are rounded, and many are flat "skipping stones" shaped by wave action in a surf zone. Where was the conglomerate deposited? Near the ocean shoreline. The rock layers at your feet are nonmarine, yet 15 feet up the cliff there is a marine conglomerate. These rock layers record flooding by the Pliocene sea. The sea-level rise may be due to a global rise in sea level or to down-dropping of the land by fault movements, or both.

CHAPTER 9
QUATERNARY HISTORY

The preceding five chapters have been introductions to the subdivisions of the Tertiary Period—that is, the epochs known as Paleocene, Eocene, Oligocene, Miocene, and Pliocene (refer to the geologic time scale in Figure 1.5, and the column of sedimentary rocks in San Diego in Figure 1.7). We turn our attention now to the youngest period, the Quaternary. It was named by Paul Desnoyers in 1829 based on rocks and fossils in the Seine River basin of France. The Quaternary is typified by fossil plants and animals similar to the organisms now living.

In 1839, Charles Lyell emended his Pliocene category by splitting off its younger portion and calling it the Pleistocene. In 1846, Edward Forbes equated the term Pleistocene with the time of the continental glaciers. In 1873, Lyell accepted Forbes' interpretation of the Pleistocene, thus changing the basis of its definition to climate.

Today's version of the geologic time scale defines a Quaternary Period made up of the Pleistocene and Holocene Epochs. The prevailing view is that Pleistocene time began 1.8 million years ago and was succeeded by the Holocene, which spans the latest 11,000 years, the time since the latest worldwide retreat of glaciers. A debate rages today about where to place the base of the Pleistocene, the Pliocene–Pleistocene boundary, which also is the Tertiary–Quaternary boundary. If we stick to the premise that Pleistocene

refers to the time of the current Ice Age, then the Pliocene–
Pleistocene boundary would be placed at 2.67 million years ago. If
this interpretation is accepted, then the redefined Pleistocene Epoch
lengthens in duration and encompasses the San Diego Formation,
changing it from Pliocene to Pleistocene.

In our study of the Quaternary history of San Diego, we will
spend most of our time looking at how the landscape has been
shaped. The two main shaping agents are high stands of sea level
wherein marine erosion cuts sea floors across San Diego and the
topographic effects of active faults.

Quaternary Rise and Fall of Sea Level

Global sea level rises and falls as worldwide glaciers retreat and
advance. In the last 2.67 million years, sea level has risen and fall-
en up to 625 feet. What do changing sea levels do to San Diego?
Ocean waves cut erosion surfaces across rocks to create sea floors,
and breaking waves attack hills to form beach cliffs (Figure 9.1).
These erosional features are distinctive; they allow us to recognize
former sea floors and cliffed coastlines. Look at E. H. Quayle's drawing of San Diego topography (Figure 9.2). Do you see former sea
floors? They are the nearly flat areas, the mesas or terraces that
stand out as white areas on the diagram—Linda Vista, San Diego,
Otay, Chula Vista, Nestor, Tia Juana. The mesas and terraces lie at
different elevations because they were formed at different times by
different sea-level highstands. Also, the same ancient sea floor may
vary in elevation due to later deformation and differential uplift
caused by faulting. There are other ancient sea floors too small for
Quayle to show on his drawing. We will visit one of the small terraces in La Jolla on our field trip.

Tectonics

Much of metropolitan San Diego is built on former sea floors because the nearly flat mesas make excellent building sites. When we
look at these mesas, do higher sea levels of the past explain their
present elevations? Not entirely. If the ice sheets on Antarctica and
Greenland were to melt, global sea level would rise about 210 feet.
But some of the mesas stand at elevations hundreds of feet higher

Figure 9.1. Sea floors and sea cliffs cut across and into Cretaceous sedimentary rocks at La Jolla Bay (a) and tip of Point Loma (b).

Figure 9.1a. La Jolla Bay.

Figure 9.1b. Point Loma.

Figure 9.2. Physiographic diagram of San Diego drawn by E. H. Quayle. From Hertlein and Grant, 1944.

yet. What else has happened to cause their elevation? The land is rising due to large-scale adjustments on a plate-tectonic scale. In the last million years, the San Diego region has been rising at an average rate of about 5.5 inches per thousand years. Moreover, in the last 80,000 years the rate of uplift seems to have increased to nearly 12 inches per thousand years, and southwest of the Rose Canyon fault the uplift rate is closer to 18 inches per thousand years. Inches of uplift occurring over thousands of years may not seem impressive at first, but remember the cardinal principle of geology—uniformitarianism. Small changes acting over long lengths of time produce major effects. To gain some perspective on this, consider that over the span of a million years, 6 inches of uplift every thousand years yields 6,000 inches (500 feet) of uplift. Thus the rising and falling sea levels have cut sea floors into San Diego at progressively lower elevations as the region has been, and continues to be, uplifted by plate-tectonic interactions.

Marine Terraces

The elevated sea floors of San Diego are some of the most impressive in the world. Let's take a closer look at how they form, how many there are, and how much fault-caused deformation they record.

FORMATION OF MARINE TERRACES AND BEACH RIDGES

Several processes combine to form a marine terrace. So far we have focused on ocean-wave erosion cutting sea floors or abrasion platforms (Figures 9.1 and 9.2). The wave-cut platform typically becomes covered by marine sediments several feet thick (Figure 9.3). When the sea retreats from its wave-cut floor, cliff erosion and local rain runoff bury the abrasion platform with nonmarine sediments, yielding topography known as a marine terrace.

Prominent topographic features associated with some of the ancient shorelines are beach ridges, which are elongate ridges of sediment built up just landward of the shoreline. Arthur Ellis mapped and described some of these beach ridges in 1919 (Figure 9.4). Look at the geometry of Tecolote Creek and its tributaries shown in Figure 9.4, and notice how the beach ridges control the stream pattern.

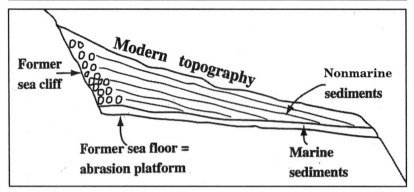

Figure 9.3. Schematic cross section through a marine terrace.

How do these beach ridges form? Arthur Ellis explained the process well:

> These ridges were formed by the waves along former shore lines just as similar ridges are now being formed along the shore . . . in a manner very similar to that in which the sand spit that extends from Coronado south to the mainland was recently formed. If the land were raised 100 feet, San Diego Bay would be entirely dry, and the sand spit would form a ridge which would have very much the appearance of the old ridges on Linda Vista Mesa. (Ellis and Lee, 1919)

One of the unfortunate effects of the growing urbanization of San Diego is the wanton disregard for the natural landscape. Beach ridges are being bulldozed and destroyed to make level lots rather than builders adapting to an interesting and significant landscape. If we look into one of the remaining beach ridges, we usually find its basal sediment layers are flat-pebble conglomerate and medium- to coarse-grained sandstones with thin parallel laminations of dark metallic grains; these sediments were deposited in the swash zone of a beach. Higher up within the ridge are found well-sorted fine sandstones with the inclined thin laminations typical of a wind-blown dune. On the landward side of some beach ridges are found mudstones made of fine silty and clayey sediments that settled out-of-water in a lagoonal setting.

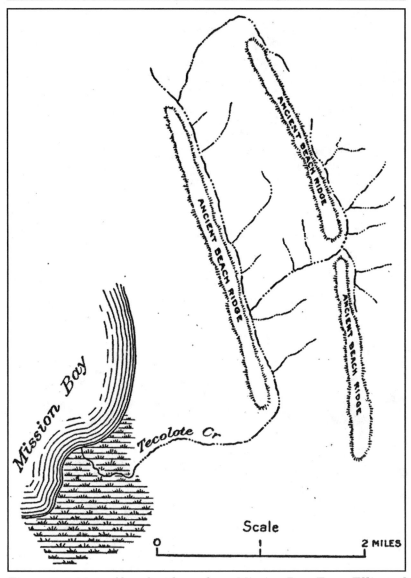

*Figure 9.4. Map of beach ridges above Mission Bay. From Ellis and
   Lee, 1919.*

Returning to Figure 9.2, you can see some beach ridges drawn by Quayle on top of the Linda Vista Mesa northeast of Mission Bay. After the former sea floors were elevated, what happened to alter them? They have been carved by running water to create the familiar valleys dividing our mesas. In sum, the dominant land shapes of urban San Diego are beach-ridge adorned, uplifted sea floors that have been thoroughly dissected by rain-water runoff that created westward-inclined canyons.

BEACH-RIDGE PALEOSOL AND PALEOCLIMATE

The beach ridges have stood as topographic highs for hundreds of thousands of years. During this Ice Age interval, the climate of San Diego has varied markedly as continental glaciers have advanced and retreated in polar regions. The beach-ridge sedimentary rocks have been significantly altered by soil-forming processes under the Pleistocene climate (Figure 9.5). Soils are alterations of surface rock

Figure 9.5. Beach ridge at Eastgate Mall north of Miramar Road. Outcrop is red and exposes soil horizons formed during maximum advances of Pleistocene glaciers.

and typically form in layers with different compositions. The beach-ridge rocks have (1) pronounced red colors due to precipitation and oxidation of iron-bearing minerals; (2) low pH readings revealing their acidity; (3) opal that has replaced some former plant roots; and (4) various soil horizons, including clay-rich layers, iron- and silica-cemented hardpans, and layers containing abundant, small-pebble-sized ironstone concretions (Figure 9.6). In the soil-forming process, clay minerals form and migrate downward along with elements such as iron and silicon. The clays, iron, and silica accumulate or precipitate in subsurface horizons or layers. In the San Diego beach ridges, the iron- and silica-cemented hardpan (*Cm* soil horizon) lies below the clay-rich layer (*Bt* horizon), which is overlain by the ironstone concretion horizon (*Bir* horizon).

Figure 9.6. Ironstone concretions in the Bir *horizon (iron-rich layer in the* B *horizon) of Pleistocene paleosol.*

Under what climatic conditions did this paleosol form? It formed in a wetter climate with acidic soil water. These ancient soils probably formed during Ice Age glacial advances when San Diego's climate was colder and wetter—more like Oregon and Washington today. With annual rainfalls of 20 to 40 inches, the sandy beach ridges were likely hosts for pine forests. The limited stands of Torrey Pines that remain in the Del Mar area today are probably the remnants of a forest that flourished under the climate of glacial maximum advance. The litter of pine needles below a grove of mature pine trees makes for highly acidic groundwater, which accentuates the alteration and decomposition in the underlying soil zone.

AGES OF SAN DIEGO MARINE TERRACES

How can the marine terraces be dated? Some of the terrace sediments contain fossils that can be correlated to the global sequence using the law of faunal succession. Fossils of solitary corals are occasionally found, and a coral contains enough radioactive elements in the uranium-decay series to allow radiometric dating. Heavy-shelled fossil clams also are found, and inside their shells is organic material that can be dated by amino-acid racemization. Putting it all together, Phil Kern and Tom Rockwell have been able to date some terraces, which, in turn, allows inferences about the ages of other terraces.

Look again at Figure 9.2. The eastern edge of Linda Vista Mesa is estimated to have been the shoreline of San Diego 1.29 million years ago. The Nestor Terrace near the Mexican border was cut by ocean waves just 120,000 years ago. The mesas and terraces of Figure 9.2 represent over a million years of work by ocean waves abrading at least 16 different platforms or sea floors.

Check Figure 9.4 again. The two beach ridges mapped in 1919 by Ellis each lie just landward of two shorelines; the eastern one formed about 795,000 years ago and the western one developed about 698,000 years ago.

DEFORMATION OF MARINE TERRACES

Figure 9.7 is a view westward from Del Cerro across the Linda Vista Mesa. Note the remarkable flatness of this elevated sea floor. Also note Mount Soledad rising up on the western horizon; it has some of the same marine terraces as Linda Vista Mesa, but they are warped upward by movements in the Rose Canyon fault zone.

Figure 9.7. View westward from Del Cerro. Note flatness of the up-lifted, ancient sea floor. Mount Soledad, visible on the hori-zon, is a part of the same sea floor but has been warped upward by the Rose Canyon fault.

How long have these faults been active? Figures 8.9, 8.10, and 8.12 (at Tourmaline Surfing Park) show that the Pliocene erosion surface dips more than the San Diego Formation sitting on top of it, which, in turn, dips more than the Pleistocene rocks above it. These variations in inclination depend on the age of the rocks and collectively suggest that the Rose Canyon fault has been active for upward of 2 million years. The Rose Canyon fault remains active and capable of generating large earthquakes today.

In 1970 Gary Peterson mapped the trends of beach ridges to gain insights into deformation history (Figure 9.8). These beach ridges formed horizontally, but now they are warped and tilted down to the south. The ages of the beach ridges shown in Figure 9.8 are Linda Vista, 855,000 years; Tecolote, 795,000 years; and Clairemont, 698,000 years. The deformation and possible truncation of beach

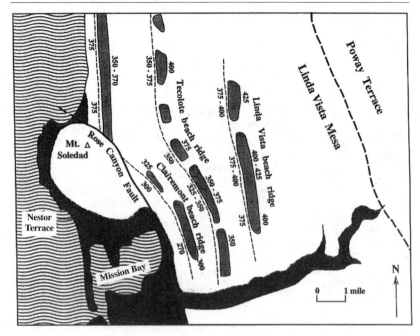

*Figure 9.8. Map of beach ridges in San Diego showing their defor-
mation (elevations in feet). Modified from Peterson, 1970.*

ridges show the Rose Canyon fault zone to have been active for hundreds of thousands of years. Also consider that the marine terraces
have been lifted all the way to the top of Mount Soledad, providing
further evidence of the long-term activity of the Rose Canyon fault
zone.

NESTOR TERRACE
The Nestor Terrace is shown near the Mexican border by Quayle in
Figure 9.2 and around Mount Soledad and Mission Bay by Peterson in Figure 9.8. Uranium-series dates from solitary corals show
that the Nestor Terrace formed 120,000 years ago during an interglacial interval with an elevated global sea level. What would San
Diego have looked like 120,000 years ago? Quite different than it
does today (Figure 9.9). Mount Soledad already stood tall, Point

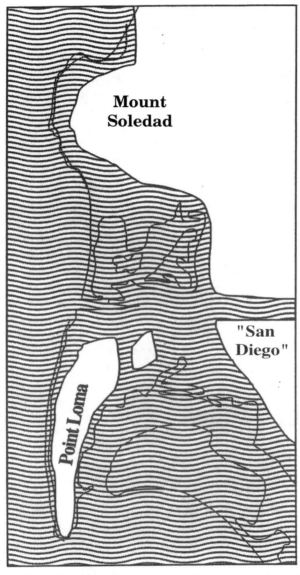

Figure 9.9. San Diego during the interglacial interval of 120,000 years ago.

Loma and Loma Portal were islands, but the elevated sea level flooded many familiar sites, such as Pacific Beach, Ocean Beach, and Coronado.

Quaternary Faulting Shapes the Land

The topography for most of the San Diego metropolitan area is reasonably simple—uplifted sea floors slope gently to the west and are dissected by west-flowing rivers carving significant canyons. This regional pattern changes west of the Rose Canyon fault zone, where Mount Soledad bends upward, Mission Bay warps downward, Point Loma rises up, and San Diego Bay is dropping down. This seemingly helter-skelter topography is logical once the geometric constraints placed by the bends in the Rose Canyon fault zone are understood.

Let's look at some basic concepts concerning strike-slip faults, that is, faults with dominantly horizontal movements. Notice in the top drawing of Figure 9.10 that a right-lateral strike-slip fault occurs when the block on the right-hand side moves horizontally toward an individual straddling the fault. For the Rose Canyon fault this occurs because the western side of the fault is riding northwestward on the Pacific plate at a faster rate than the eastern side.

Next look at the middle drawing of Figure 9.10 and mentally place yourself opposite a bend or kink in the fault. Notice that when the left-hand length of a crooked right-lateral fault is stepped closer to you, it creates a zone of compression or uplift at the bend in the fault. In the bottom drawing in Figure 9.10, notice that when the right-hand side of a bent right-lateral fault lies closer to you, it creates a zone of tension or pulling apart at the bend in the fault.

MOUNT SOLEDAD AND MISSION BAY

The preceding theoretical interpretations of fault geometry were applied to the Rose Canyon fault zone in 1970 by George Moore and Mike Kennedy. Let's apply these concepts to the major faults in San Diego (refer to the map in Figure 9.11). Notice that after the northwest-southeast trending Rose Canyon fault comes ashore at La Jolla, its path becomes more east-west until it reaches Rose Canyon where it resumes its northwest-southeast orientation. When the Rose Canyon fault zone in La Jolla is viewed from the side, it is

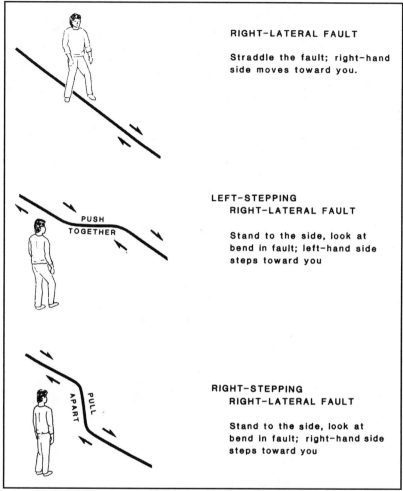

RIGHT-LATERAL FAULT

Straddle the fault; right-hand side moves toward you.

LEFT-STEPPING
RIGHT-LATERAL FAULT

Stand to the side, look at bend in fault; left-hand side steps toward you

RIGHT-STEPPING
RIGHT-LATERAL FAULT

Stand to the side, look at bend in fault; right-hand side steps toward you

Figure 9.10. Strike-slip faults and the processes at their bends.

seen to have a prominent left step. In theory, this setting should produce uplift. In reality, there rises Mount Soledad. What is happening in La Jolla? The western side of the Rose Canyon fault zone is carrying La Jolla northwestward. When it reaches the left step just south of Ardath Road, its movement is hindered. The

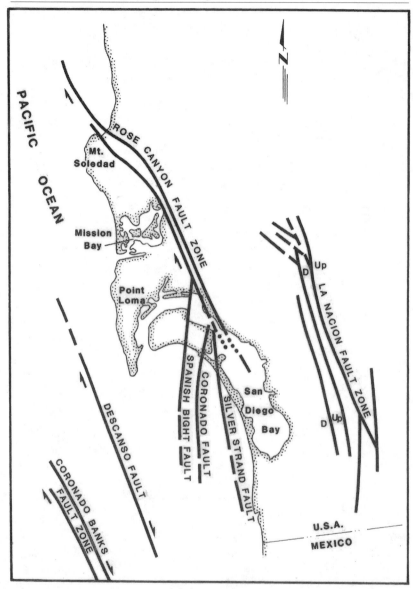

Figure 9.11. Major faults in urban and near-offshore San Diego.

resultant compression pushes the sedimentary rock layers against the bend, causing folding (Figure 9.12); this process is somewhat analogous to the stacking up of railroad cars in a collision.

Figure 9.12 is a north-south oriented cross section drawn as a vertical slice from Mount Soledad southward through Point Loma. At Mount Soledad the cross section shows steeply tilted sedimentary strata compressed into an anticlinal fold. The compressional folding is further shown by the downwarp forming the topographic low that is filled with seawater to make Mission Bay.

The uplifting effect at the fault bend also is shown by the exposure of late Cretaceous sandstone, mudstone, and conglomerate beds in the sea cliffs of La Jolla, Bird Rock, and Point Loma. These rocks formed 76 to 72 million years ago and are deeply buried elsewhere in San Diego, but because of the compression at the left-stepping fault bend in La Jolla, the Cretaceous rocks are being lifted above sea level for us to enjoy.

SAN DIEGO BAY

When the Rose Canyon fault zone is followed southward, it seems to die out in San Diego Bay. The seismic activity apparently transfers to the short, north-trending Silver Strand, Coronado, and Spanish Bight faults heading offshore toward the Descanso fault (Figure 9.11). According to Mark Legg, the northern end of the Descanso fault lies offshore from Point Loma. Working from a research ship, Legg has traced the Descanso fault southward to where it comes back onshore south of Ensenada and merges into the Agua Blanca fault zone.

Taking a side view in Figure 9.11, examine the geometric relations between the Rose Canyon and Descanso faults. The Rose Canyon fault zone appears to end in San Diego Bay. The tectonic pressures are then passed through a major right step with transfer of movement to the offshore Descanso fault. In theory, this right step should produce a pull-apart basin. In reality, there is San Diego Bay.

The right step between the ends of the right-lateral Rose Canyon and Descanso fault zones creates a releasing bend, causing the rocks to be stretched apart and dropped down. In response to this

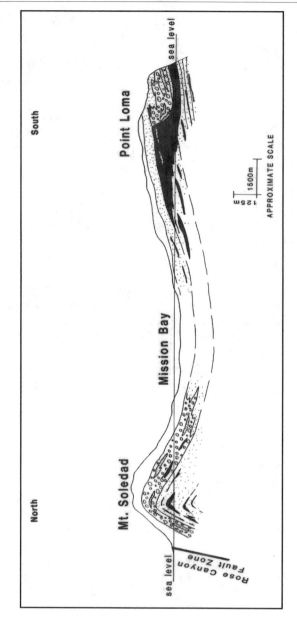

Figure 9.12. North–south-oriented cross section showing sedimentary rock layers folded by compression at the La Jolla left step in the Rose Canyon fault zone.

stretching the rocks do not deform elastically; instead they respond with brittle failure as faults. Specifically, the down dropping of the San Diego Bay region has been accommodated by a series of down-to-the-basin faults with dominantly vertical offsets—namely, the La Nacion fault zone. A typical fault in the La Nacion system has suffered a vertical drop on its western side in reaction to the sinking of the San Diego Bay basin.

COASTAL TOPOGRAPHY

The large-scale topographic elements of San Diego west of the Rose Canyon fault zone are directly attributable to movements along the faults (Figure 9.13). There also are numerous smaller-scale topographic features resulting from movements on faults of the Rose Canyon system. George Moore called attention to the shape of the coastline at La Jolla. The relatively smooth and arcuate coastline from Oceanside to La Jolla Shores beach takes a prominent westward jump to La Jolla Cove, as shown in Figures 9.11 and 9.13. This physiographic discontinuity is consistent with a few miles of northward movement on the west side of the Rose Canyon fault zone.

Notice also on Figure 9.13 that North Island and Coronado Island were once separate landmasses divided by bay water filling the elongate feature called Spanish Bight. See Figure 9.11 for a picture of why Spanish Bight existed—the Bight was eroded through ground-up rock debris along the Spanish Bight fault. But the U.S. Navy filled in the Bight to create more land. Did this burial of the fault end its earthquake-generating potential? In 1985 and 1986, numerous earthquakes occurred on these north-south oriented faults crossing Coronado, including a magnitude 4.7 earthquake on 29 October 1986.

Quaternary Field Trip: Out and About in La Jolla

On this field trip we will visit five separate localities (Figure 9.14). The first stop is on top of Mount Soledad, my favorite geological view site in San Diego. The other four stops can be done in any order you choose, even on different days. Pick a day following a

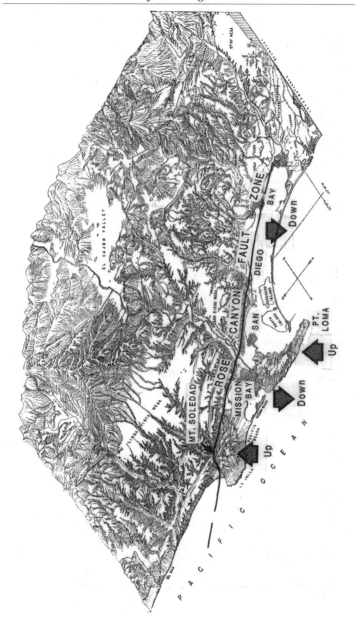

Figure 9.13. Coastal topography caused by bends in the Rose Canyon fault zone — a left step in La Jolla and a right step across San Diego Bay.

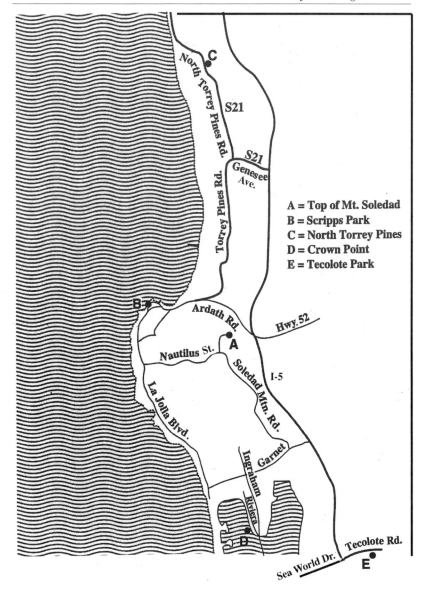

Figure 9.14. Map for field trip out and about in La Jolla.

rainfall or during a Santa Ana weather condition and enjoy the view from the memorial cross atop Mount Soledad (*Thomas Guide*, p. 1227, J7).

THE VIEW: TOP OF MOUNT SOLEDAD

What a beautiful view site! There is so much to observe and learn up here. Sweep your eyes across the entire horizon and drink in the landscape. Refer to Figure 9.2 for orientation and some place names.

- Notice the preponderance of flat-topped mesas (the Spanish word *mesa* means table)—these are uplifted sea floors. Rainwater running off the raised sea floors has cut impressive canyons.
- Look to the northeast and find the runways at Miramar Marine Corps Air Station near the eastern edge of Linda Vista Mesa. Do you see the ancient sea cliffs farther east, beyond the airfield? The sea cliffs are parallel to and east of Interstate 15. These ancient sea cliffs are analogous to the present-day sea cliffs running from Torrey Pines to La Jolla Shores. When were the ancient sea cliffs cut by ocean waves? Over 1 million years ago.
- Run your eyes north to south, and back again, over the path of the Rose Canyon fault zone (use Figures 9.11 and 9.13 to help locate the fault zone). Notice the following topographic effects of the faults: The mesas stop where they are chopped off at the fault zone—Clairemont drops down through Bay Park to Mission Bay, and Mission Hills drops down through Old Town to San Diego Bay. The fault zone is wide enough to include part of the University of San Diego campus, the Presidio, and Old Town before passing into downtown San Diego where the faults are hard to locate because big buildings cover most of the ground. Some of the faults pass beneath the San Diego–Coronado Bay Bridge before ending in San Diego Bay.
- Do you sense the prominent left step in the fault zone? You are standing within the fault bend; its northern side lies north of you, yet south of nearby Ardath Road. This left step in the Rose Canyon fault zone has caused the uplift of the earth beneath your feet (Figure 9.12). Looking south you can see where the land warps down and passes beneath the waters of Mission Bay.

- Look east and find Highway 52 running westward toward you through San Clemente Canyon. Now look east up the canyon and let your eyes follow its stream westward. What happens to the stream when it nears Mount Soledad? It turns and takes a 115-degree bend to the southeast down Rose Canyon. Why would a westward-flowing stream, after almost reaching the ocean, take such a radical turn? The stream course probably was blocked by the rising Mount Soledad.

- Where is the most active fault in the Rose Canyon fault zone? It is the Mount Soledad fault; it passes immediately south of where you are now standing. Look south down Rose Canyon toward the canyon mouth and find the Santa Fe Street bridge crossing over and leading onto Interstate 5. Mentally draw a line from just south of where you are standing and connect it to the east side of the Santa Fe Street bridge; you have just drawn the path of the active Mount Soledad fault. (For precise locations of faults, see the La Jolla quadrangle map by Mike Kennedy, 1975.) In 1991 Tom Rockwell and Scott Lindvall trenched the active fault down by Santa Fe Street in the San Diego Gas and Electric Company parking lot. With the help of students Colleen Haradan, Kenji Hirabayashi, and Liz Baker, they measured a minimum of 29 feet of right-lateral movement occurring in the last 8,155 years. Is the fault still active and dangerous? Yes.

- Look south and see the fault-raised block of Point Loma. Remember it has been an island numerous times in the last 2 million years, for example, see Figure 9.9. Why is Point Loma no longer an island? How did it become tied to mainland San Diego? The San Diego River has been depositing its sands and muds as a delta building westward, splitting the bay into two parts—Mission and San Diego. Westward growth of the delta has constructed a land bridge to Point Loma. What is the age of the delta? It began forming after the latest sea-level rise, so it is less than 11,000 years old. What will happen to the river delta sediments during a large earthquake on the Rose Canyon fault? The water-saturated sediments will undergo liquefaction. When the foundation earth flows during liquefaction, rigid structures built by humans may fail.

- Look south and see Mission Beach. How old is Mission Beach? Less than 11,000 years. How did it form? Following the latest glacial retreat, sea level rose to near its present location. Then, ocean waves from the northern Pacific Ocean pushed beach sand southward to build a sand spit, which we call Mission Beach.
- Look south and compare the amount of beach sand at South Mission Beach to the amount at Ocean Beach. Why is there so much beach sand at South Mission Beach and so little at Ocean Beach? The Mission Bay jetties block the southward flow of beach sand, depriving Ocean Beach and Sunset Cliffs of most of their beach sand supply. What harm comes to Ocean Beach and Sunset Cliffs from a lessened supply of beach sand? Instead of crashing on beach sand, big ocean waves now beat on sea cliffs, causing faster erosion. The City of San Diego has responded by building cement walls to cover natural cliffs and by burying beach coves beneath big ugly rocks to slow down the inevitable erosion.
- If the air is clear enough, look far to the south-southeast and see the Silver Strand, the sand bar connecting Coronado to Imperial Beach. Is the Silver Strand natural or human made? It is a natural feature built by late summer ocean waves coming from the south. The northward-moving waves carry sand northward from the Tijuana River delta to build the Silver Strand.
- Look south to San Diego Bay. Chapter 1 began with the Portuguese explorer Juan Cabrillo sailing into San Diego Bay in 1542—an historic event. But now you have a more powerful understanding of this event that allows a more accurate description. In 1542, Cabrillo sailed into the seawater-filled pull-apart basin created at the right step where the right-lateral Rose Canyon fault system transfers its movement offshore to the Descanso fault. Were it not for the lands pushed up and warped down by our active faults, Cabrillo's memorable landing could not have occurred—this is geologic control of history.

SCRIPPS PARK AT LA JOLLA COVE

Scripps Park is as pretty as it gets (Figure 9.15; and *Thomas Guide,* p. 1227, E6 and F6). It is the quintessential little beach park and is known around the world. How did geologic processes help here?

Figure 9.15. View of Scripps Park at La Jolla Cove. This park is part of the Bird Rock Terrace that was cut during a sea-level lowstand 80,000 years ago.

The park sits on a segment of the Bird Rock Terrace. It was cut by ocean waves 80,000 years ago when sea level was about 45 feet *lower* than today and sea-water temperatures were colder.

- How could this terrace have been cut by a sea level lower than today but be well above sea level today? The land here has risen nearly 12 inches per thousand years for the last 80,000 years, thus lifting the terrace above sea level for our recreational pleasures.
- Why were ocean waters colder 80,000 years ago? Sea level was lower because a tremendous volume of water had been evaporated to build the polar ice sheets, which, in turn, lowered water temperatures.
- If you look into fractures in the overhanging cliff rocks at Boomer Beach you can find fossiliferous sands that flowed down into fractures and filled them when the area was still below sea level.

NORTH TORREY PINES ROADCUT

An east-facing roadcut on North Torrey Pines Road (S21) presents an intriguing geological cross section for your puzzle-solving pleasure. Drive northbound in the right-hand lane about halfway down the slope to Torrey Pines State Beach (*Thomas Guide,* p. 1207, H2). When you see the roadcut pictured in Figure 9.16, pull off the road to the right, park your car, and ready yourself for an intellectual treat. Do not cross the road, or even stand near it, but back off safely eastward and contemplate the rock exposures—Eocene Torrey Sandstone is overlain by Pleistocene sedimentary rocks, but their history has been enriched by the cutting and filling of a submarine canyon as well as by faulting. Your task is to recognize these ancient events and organize them in chronological order from oldest to youngest. Are you ready?

Figure 9.16. East-facing roadcut on North Torrey Pines Road about halfway down the slope to Torrey Pines State Beach. Eocene tidally influenced sandstones are overlain by Pleistocene sedimentary rocks, including a sediment-filled submarine canyon. A fault cuts through some of the rocks.

- Define the extent of the Eocene Torrey Sandstone. We looked at these tidal-influenced sedimentary rocks on the Eocene field trip walking the beach from Torrey Pines to Scripps Pier (Chapter 5). The Eocene rocks are at the bottom of the roadcut, are lighter colored, and more resistant to erosion.
- Now recognize the more easily eroded, reddish-orangish Pleistocene sedimentary rocks high up on the roadcut. Find the contact between the Eocene and Pleistocene rocks. What is the nature of their contact? An unconformity. Do you see the evidence of this erosion surface? Looking uphill, the ancient erosion is subtle; but looking downhill, it is evident that the erosion carved out a small submarine canyon, later filled by sediments. Do you see the former submarine canyon? One wall is shown on the right-hand side of Figure 9.16. The Pleistocene submarine canyon is filled with marine sediments, but some of the overlying reddish sediments are nonmarine. You are seeing varying sedimentary responses to falling and rising sea levels as continental ice sheets grew and shrank.
- Now analyze the fault shown on the left side of Figure 9.16. Does it have dominantly vertical or horizontal movement? Vertical. Did it form in response to compressive or tensional forces? Tensional. Can you see the pulling apart that occurred at the fault with some rock debris falling down into the fault? Is the fault still active? No—the upper rock layers are not offset.
- Do you see the cannonball concretions, the purplish-brown resistant cemented-sandstone masses in the Eocene Torrey Sandstone? How did the concretions form? They grew in the past, below the groundwater table, as ions migrated toward nuclei and precipitated as cement between sand grains, creating an enlarging ball of cemented sandstone. Are these hard concretions still growing here today? No.

CROWN POINT AND PLEISTOCENE FOSSILS

Crown Point juts into northern Mission Bay and divides it into two areas (Figure 9.14). The northwestern water body is Sail Bay, and its southeastern shore, below Riviera Drive, has interesting rock layers (*Thomas Guide,* p. 1268, A1). Exposed in the low cliffs are some richly fossiliferous Pleistocene sedimentary rocks (Figure 9.17). These medium- and coarse-grained sandstones are named the Bay Point Formation. How energetic was the Pleistocene marine water here? It was a high-energy environment as shown by (1) the coarse grain sizes, (2) the ancient U-shaped channel bottoms, (3) the cross bedding or inclined layers of sand grains that slid down the fronts of former submarine sand dunes, and (4) the abundant heavy-shelled invertebrate fossils. In some rock layers the fossils are more abundant than the sand grains—geologists call a rock made mostly of shells a *coquina*. Can you visualize the Pleistocene depositional environment here? High-energy tidal currents carried away fine sediments, leaving behind what we see today—coarse sands and abundant heavy shells of marine invertebrate organisms.

Figure 9.17. Richly fossiliferous Pleistocene sedimentary rocks near southwestern tip of Crown Point.

TECOLOTE COMMUNITY PARK FEATURING A ROSE CANYON FAULT

The Rose Canyon faults occur in a zone covering a linear swath two-thirds of a mile wide. (See the geologic maps of the La Jolla and

Point Loma quadrangles done by Mike Kennedy in Kennedy and Peterson, 1975.) A good location to see and feel one of the faults occurs in the north-facing cliff behind the left-centerfield fence of the upper baseball field in Tecolote Community Park (Figure 9.18; and *Thomas Guide,* p. 1268, F2). Not only is this a good geologic site, but up-canyon one-eighth of a mile lies an interesting nature center staffed by park rangers. Check it out—you'll like it.

- Walk to centerfield, and face south to view the fault. On your left (east) are marine layers of fine sandstone and mudstone of the Eocene Scripps Formation. On your right are Pleistocene conglomerate overlying well-sorted fine sandstones of the Pliocene San Diego Formation. Due to ongoing erosion, you may have to dig a bit to expose the San Diego Formation or walk westward along the outcrop to see it.

Figure 9.18. One of the Rose Canyon faults exposed behind the left-centerfield fence of the upper baseball field in Tecolote Community Park. Fault separates Eocene Scripps Formation on left (east) from Pliocene San Diego and Pleistocene Bay Point Formations on right (west).

- As you face the fault, can you tell which side has moved down? The west (right) side. Use the law of superposition to understand why west-side down is the correct answer. The Rose Canyon fault zone contains strike-slip faults with dominantly horizontal movements. How much horizontal movement has occurred here? The amount of horizontal movement is difficult to impossible to assess just standing in front of this two-dimensional vertical face. Are you looking at an active fault? Yes. It may not feel scary or threatening just looking at this small fracture in the cliff, but this is it, the real deal—an active fault.

REFERENCES

Abbott, P. L. 1981. Cenozoic paleosols, San Diego area, California. *Catena,* v. 8, p. 223–37.

Abbott, P. L., and T. E. Smith. 1978. Trace-element comparison of clasts in Eocene conglomerates, southwestern California and northwestern Mexico. *Journal of Geology,* v. 86, p. 753–62.

———. 1989. Sonora, Mexico, source for the Eocene Poway conglomerate of southern California. *Geology,* v. 17, p. 329–32.

Abbott, P. L., R. P. Kies, D. Krummenacher, and D. Martin. 1983. Potassium-argon ages of rhyolitic bedrock and conglomerate clasts in Eocene strata, northwestern Mexico and southern California. In *Tectonics and sedimentation along faults of the San Andreas system,* ed. D. W. Andersen and M. J. Rymer., p. 59–66. Pacific Section, Society of Economic Paleontologists and Mineralogists.

Abbott, P. L., J. A. Minch, and G. L. Peterson. 1976. Pre-Eocene paleosol south of Tijuana, Mexico. *Journal of Sedimentary Petrology,* v. 46, p. 355–61.

Balch, D. C., S. Hosken Bartling, and P. L. Abbott. 1984. Volcaniclastic strata of the Upper Jurassic Santiago Peak Volcanics, San Diego County, California. In *Tectonics and sedimentation along the California margin,* ed. J. K. Crouch and S. B. Bachman, p. 157–70. Pacific Section, Society of Economic Paleontologists and Mineralogists.

Bartling, W. A., and P. L. Abbott. 1983. Upper Cretaceous sedimentation and tectonics with reference to the Eocene, San Miguel Island and San Diego area, California. In *Cenozoic marine sedimentation, Pacific margin, U.S.A.,* ed. D. K. Larue and R. J. Steel, p. 133–50. Pacific Section, Society of Economic Paleontologists and Mineralogists.

Berry, R. W. 1991. Deposition of Eocene and Oligocene bentonites and their relationship to Tertiary tectonics, San Diego County. In *Eocene geologic history, San Diego region,* ed. P. L. Abbott and J. A. May, v. 68, p. 107–13. Pacific Section, Society of Economic Paleontologists and Mineralogists.

Cleveland, G. B. 1960. Geology of the Otay bentonite deposit, San Diego County, California. *California Division of Mines Special Report,* v. 64, 16 p.

Deméré, T. A. 1981. Fossil whales of San Diego. *Environment Southwest,* no. 492, p. 17–20; and no. 493, p. 22–25.

————. 1983. The Neogene San Diego basin: A review of the marine Pliocene San Diego Formation. In *Cenozoic marine sedimentation, Pacific margin, U.S.A.,* ed. D. K. Larue and R. J. Steel, p. 187–95. Pacific Section, Society of Economic Paleontologists and Mineralogists.

————. 1986. EastLake: A new chapter in the geologic history of San Diego County. *Environment Southwest,* no. 515, p. 9–13.

————. 1988. An armored dinosaur from Carlsbad. *Environment Southwest,* no. 523, p. 12–15.

Eisenberg, L. I. 1985. Depositional processes in the landward part of an Eocene tidal lagoon, northern San Diego County. In *On the manner of deposition of the Eocene strata in northern San Diego County,* ed. P. L. Abbott, p. 55–68. San Diego Association of Geologists Guidebook.

Ellis, A. J., and C. H. Lee. 1919. Geology and ground waters of the western part of San Diego County, California. Washington, D.C.: U. S. Geological Survey, Water-Supply Paper 446, 321 p.

Fife, D. L., J. A. Minch, and P. J. Crampton. 1967. Late Jurassic age of the Santiago Peak Volcanics, California. *Geological Society of America Bulletin,* v. 78, p. 299–304.

Frost, E. G., M. J. Fattahipour, and K. L. Robinson. 1996. Neogene detachment and strike-slip faulting in the Salton Trough region. In *Field Trip Guidebook,* ed. P. L. Abbott and J. D. Cooper, bk. 80, p. 263–76. Pacific Section, Society of Economic Paleontologists and Mineralogists.

Gottfried, M. D. 1982. Fossil fishes of the San Diego Formation. *Environment Southwest,* no. 498, p. 23–25.

Grant, U. S., IV, and H. R. Gale. 1931. Catalogue of the marine Pliocene and Pleistocene mollusca of California and adjacent regions. Memoir I. San Diego Society of Natural History, 1,036 p.

Hertlein, L. G., and U. S. Grant IV. 1944. The geology and paleontology of the marine Pliocene of San Diego, California, part 1, geology. Memoir II. San Diego Society of Natural History, 72 p. and 18 plates.

Kennedy, M. P., and G. W. Moore. 1971. Stratigraphic relations of Upper Cretaceous and Eocene formations, San Diego coastal area, California. *American Association of Petroleum Geologists Bulletin,* v. 55, p. 709–28.

Kennedy, M. P., and G. L. Peterson. 1975. Geology of the San Diego metropolitan area. Bulletin 200. Sacramento: California Division of Mines and Geology, 56 p. and 6 maps.

Kennedy, M. P., and S. S. Tan. 1977. Geology of National City, Imperial Beach, and Otay Mesa quadrangles, southern San Diego metropolitan area, California. Map Sheet 29. Sacramento: California Division of Mines and Geology.

Kern, J. P., and T. K. Rockwell. 1992. Chronology and deformation of Quaternary marine shorelines, San Diego County, California. In *Quaternary coasts of the United States,* Special Pub. 48, p. 377–82. Tulsa, Oklahoma: Society of Economic Paleontologists and Mineralogists.

Kern, J. P., and J. E. Warme. 1974. Trace fossils and bathymetry of the Upper Cretaceous Point Loma Formation, San Diego, California. *Geological Society of America Bulletin,* v. 85, p. 893–900.

Kerr, D. R. 1984. Early Neogene continental sedimentation in the Vallecito and Fish Creek Mountains, western Salton Trough, California. *Sedimentary Geology,* v. 38, p. 217–46.

Kerr, D. R., and P. L. Abbott. 1996. Miocene subaerial sturzstrom deposits, Split Mountain, Anza-Borrego Desert State Park. In *Sturzstroms and detachment faults, Anza-Borrego Desert State Park,* ed. P. L. Abbott and D. C. Seymour, bk. 24, p. 149–63. Santa Ana, California: South Coast Geological Society.

Kies, R. P., and P. L. Abbott. 1982. Sedimentology and paleogeography of lower Paleogene conglomerates, southern California continental borderland. In *Geology and mineral wealth of the California Transverse Ranges,* ed. D. L. Fife and J. A. Minch, p. 337–49. Santa Ana, California: South Coast Geological Society.

— — —. 1983. Rhyolite clast populations and tectonics in the California continental borderland. *Journal of Sedimentary Petrology,* v. 53, p. 461–75.

Lohmar, J. M., J. A. May, J. E. Boyer, and J. E. Warme. 1979. Shelf-edge deposits of the San Diego embayment. In *Eocene depositional systems, San Diego,* ed. P. L. Abbott, p. 15–27. Pacific Section, Society of Economic Paleontologists and Mineralogists.

May, J. A., J. M. Lohmar, J. E. Warme, and S. Morgan. 1991. Early to middle Eocene La Jolla Group of Black's Beach, La Jolla, California. In *Eocene geologic history, San Diego region,* ed. P. L. Abbott and J. A. May, v. 68, p. 27–36. Pacific Section, Society of Economic Paleontologists and Mineralogists

Minch, J. A. 1972. The Late Mesozoic–Early Cenozoic framework of continental sedimentation, northern Peninsular Ranges, Baja California, Mexico. Ph.D. diss., University of California, Riverside, 192 p.

Nilsen, T. H., and P. L. Abbott. 1981. Paleogeography and sedimentology of Upper Cretaceous turbidites, San Diego, California. *American Association of Petroleum Geologists Bulletin,* v. 65, p. 1256–84.

Peterson, G. L. 1970. Quaternary deformation of the San Diego area, southwestern California. In *Pacific slope geology of northern Baja California and adjacent Alta California,* ed. E. C. Allison and others, p. 120–26. Pacific Section, American Association of Petroleum Geologists.

— — —. 1979. Salt weathering textures in Eocene conglomerates, southwestern California. In *Eocene depositional systems, San Diego,* ed. P. L. Abbott, p. 115–18. Pacific Section, Society of Economic Paleontologists and Mineralogists.

Peterson, G. L., and P. L. Abbott. 1979. Mid-Eocene climatic change, southwestern California and northwestern Baja California. *Palaeogeography, Palaeoclimatology, Palaeoecology,* v. 26, p. 73–87.

Peterson, G. L., and C. E. Nordstrom. 1970. Sub-La Jolla unconformity in vicinity of San Diego, California. *American Association of Petroleum Geologists Bulletin,* v. 54, p. 265–74.

Prothero, D. R. 1991. Magnetic stratigraphy of Eocene and
Oligocene mammal localities in southern San Diego County.
In *Eocene geologic history, San Diego region,* ed. P. L. Abbott
and J. A. May, v. 68, p. 125–30. Pacific Section, Society of
Economic Paleontologists and Mineralogists.

Rockwell, T. K., S. C. Lindvall, C. C. Haraden, C. K. Hirabayashi,
and E. Baker. 1991. Minimum Holocene slip rate for the Rose
Canyon fault in San Diego, California. In *Environmental perils,
San Diego region,* ed. P. L. Abbott and W. J. Elliott, p. 37–46.
San Diego Association of Geologists.

Steer, B. L., and P. L. Abbott. 1984. Paleohydrology of the Eocene
Ballena Gravels, San Diego County, California. *Sedimentary
Geology,* v. 38, p. 181–216.

Stuart, C. J., ed., 1979. *Miocene lithofacies and depositional
environments, coastal California and northwestern Baja
California.* Pacific Section, Society of Economic Paleontologists and Mineralogists, 138 p.

Udden, J. A. 1898. Mechanical composition of wind deposits.
Augustana Library Publication 1, p. 1–69.

Vanderhurst, W. L., R. J. McCarthy, and D. L. Hannan. 1982.
Black's Beach landslide, January, 1982. In *Geologic studies in
San Diego,* ed. P. L. Abbott, p. 46–58. San Diego Association of
Geologists.

Walsh, S. L., and T. A. Deméré. 1991. Age and stratigraphy of the
Sweetwater and Otay formations, San Diego County, California. In *Eocene geologic history, San Diego region,* ed. P. L.
Abbott and J. A. May, v. 68, p. 131–48. Pacific Section, Society
of Economic Paleontologists and Mineralogists.

Wentworth, C. K. 1922. A scale of grade and class terms for clastic
sediments. *Journal of Geology,* v. 30, p. 377–92.

Woodford, A. O., E. E. Welday, and R. Merriam. 1968. Siliceous
tuff clasts in the upper Paleogene of southern California.
Geological Society of America Bulletin, v. 79, p. 1461–86.

INDEX